MILITARY MILLIONAIRE
90-DAY PLANNER

Copyright © 2022 FMTM LLC

All rights reserved. No part of this publication may be reproduced, distributed, or transmitted in any form or by any means, including photocopying, recording, or other electronic or mechanical methods, without the prior written permission of the publisher, except in the case of brief quotations embodied in critical reviews and certain other noncommercial uses permitted by copyright law. For permission requests, write to the publisher, addressed "Attention: Permissions Coordinator," at the address below.

ISBN: 978-1-7367530-4-0

All content reflects our opinion at a given time and can change as time progresses. All information should be taken as an opinion and should not be misconstrued for professional or legal advice. The contents of this book are informational in nature and are not legal or tax advice and the authors and publishers are not engaged in the provision of legal, tax, or any other advice. The views presented in this book are those of the author and do not necessarily represent the views of DoD or its components.
Front cover image and Book Design by 100Covers

Printed by FMTM LLC in the United States of America.

First printing edition 2021.

3220 S Valley View Ave
Springfield, MO 65804

www.frommilitarytomillionaire.com

THIS PLANNER BELONGS TO

_____

_____

_____

BEFORE YOU START...
BE SURE YOU CHECKOUT OUR VIDEOS ON HOW TO GET
THE MOST OUT OF THIS JOURNAL:

Or visit:
https://www.frommilitarytomillionaire.com/journal-instructions/

GOAL SETTING

THREE-YEAR GOAL

FUTURE DATE:

REVENUE:

PROFIT:

HOW YOU'LL FEEL:

ONE-YEAR GOAL

FUTURE DATE:

REVENUE:

PROFIT:

HOW YOU'LL FEEL:

REVIEW PREVIOUS QUARTER

SUMMARY

_____
_____
_____
_____
_____
_____
_____

KEY PERFORMANCE INDICATORS

TARGET	ACTUAL	NOTES

GOAL OVERVIEW

GOAL	ISSUES	NOTES
COMPLETED?	

BIGGEST OBSTACLES

OBSTACLE:
CORE OF THE PROBLEM:
BRAINSTORM SOLUTIONS:

ACTION PLAN:
WHO: DUE DATE:

OBSTACLE:
CORE OF THE PROBLEM:
BRAINSTORM SOLUTIONS:

ACTION PLAN:
WHO: DUE DATE:

OBSTACLE:
CORE OF THE PROBLEM:
BRAINSTORM SOLUTIONS:

ACTION PLAN:
WHO: DUE DATE:

UNTAPPED OPPORTUNITIES

OPPORTUNITY:

POTENTIAL REVENUE/NOI	RESOURCES & RISKS	OPPORTUNITY COST

QUARTERLY PLANNING

TASKERS

Write down any and all tasks you'd like to complete in the next 90 days:

-
-
-
-
-
-
-
-
-
-
-
-
-
-
-
-
-
-
-
-
-
-
-
-
-
-
-
-
-
-
-
-
-
-

Review all tasks and put a star next to the top 3-7 priorities. Those are now your quarterly goals.

QUARTERLY GOALS

GOAL:

WHO: DUE DATE:

SUB TASKS: PRIORITY

GOAL:

WHO: DUE DATE:

SUB TASKS: PRIORITY

GOAL:

WHO: DUE DATE:

SUB TASKS: PRIORITY

GOAL:

WHO: DUE DATE:

SUB TASKS: PRIORITY

QUARTERLY GOALS

GOAL:

WHO: DUE DATE:

SUB TASKS: PRIORITY

GOAL:

WHO: DUE DATE:

SUB TASKS: PRIORITY

GOAL:

WHO: DUE DATE:

SUB TASKS: PRIORITY

Number your quarterly goals in order of importance. 1-3 are your weekly and daily goals, and 4-7 will get moved in as you achieve the first three goals. Think of these as "bonus goals".

STRATEGIC PLAN BY WEEK

Reverse engineer your goals to figure out what tasks need to be completed each week in order to hit your deadline(s).

WEEK OF:
FOCUS | PRIORITIES
- _____
- _____
- _____
- _____
- _____
- _____

WEEK OF:
FOCUS | PRIORITIES
- _____
- _____
- _____
- _____
- _____
- _____

WEEK OF:
FOCUS | PRIORITIES
- _____
- _____
- _____
- _____
- _____
- _____

WEEK OF:
FOCUS | PRIORITIES
- _____
- _____
- _____
- _____
- _____
- _____

WEEK OF:
FOCUS | PRIORITIES
- _____
- _____
- _____
- _____
- _____
- _____

VISION

COMPANY/VENTURE

MISSION

TACTICAL ADVANTAGE

CORE VALUES

1
2
3
4
5

5-10 YEAR ULTIMATE GOAL (THINK BIG)

STRATEGIC PLAN BY WEEK

WEEK OF:

FOCUS | PRIORITIES
- _____
- _____
- _____

- _____
- _____
- _____

WEEK OF:

FOCUS | PRIORITIES
- _____
- _____
- _____

- _____
- _____
- _____

WEEK OF:

FOCUS | PRIORITIES
- _____
- _____
- _____

- _____
- _____
- _____

WEEK OF:

FOCUS | PRIORITIES
- _____
- _____
- _____

- _____
- _____
- _____

WEEK OF:

FOCUS | PRIORITIES
- _____
- _____
- _____

- _____
- _____
- _____

WEEK OF:

FOCUS | PRIORITIES
- _____
- _____
- _____

- _____
- _____
- _____

STRATEGIC PLAN BY WEEK

WEEK OF:

FOCUS | PRIORITIES
- _____
- _____
- _____

- _____
- _____
- _____

WEEK OF:

FOCUS | PRIORITIES
- _____
- _____
- _____

- _____
- _____
- _____

FITNESS/HEALTH GOALS
THIS QUARTER: _____

RELATIONSHIP GOALS
THIS QUARTER: _____

PARENTING GOALS
THIS QUARTER: _____

SAVING GOALS
THIS QUARTER: _____

INVESTING GOALS
THIS QUARTER: _____

SPIRITUAL/EMOTIONAL GOALS
THIS QUARTER: _____

PERSONAL DEVELOPMENT GOALS
THIS QUARTER: _____

NOTES AND BRAINSTORMING

NOTES AND BRAINSTORMING

MONTHLY ACTION PLAN

MONTHLY PLAN

JAN FEB MAR APR MAY JUN JUL AUG SEP OCT NOV DEC

SUNDAY	MONDAY	TUESDAY	WEDNESDAY
SUNDAY	MONDAY	TUESDAY	WEDNESDAY
SUNDAY	MONDAY	TUESDAY	WEDNESDAY
SUNDAY	MONDAY	TUESDAY	WEDNESDAY
SUNDAY	MONDAY	TUESDAY	WEDNESDAY

NOTES

FOCUS:

THURSDAY	FRIDAY	SATURDAY	TASKS
THURSDAY	FRIDAY	SATURDAY	TASKS
THURSDAY	FRIDAY	SATURDAY	TASKS
THURSDAY	FRIDAY	SATURDAY	TASKS
THURSDAY	FRIDAY	SATURDAY	TASKS

NOTES

MONTHLY PLAN

JAN FEB MAR APR MAY JUN JUL AUG SEP OCT NOV DEC

SUNDAY	MONDAY	TUESDAY	WEDNESDAY
SUNDAY	MONDAY	TUESDAY	WEDNESDAY
SUNDAY	MONDAY	TUESDAY	WEDNESDAY
SUNDAY	MONDAY	TUESDAY	WEDNESDAY
SUNDAY	MONDAY	TUESDAY	WEDNESDAY

NOTES

FOCUS:

THURSDAY	FRIDAY	SATURDAY	TASKS
THURSDAY	FRIDAY	SATURDAY	TASKS
THURSDAY	FRIDAY	SATURDAY	TASKS
THURSDAY	FRIDAY	SATURDAY	TASKS
THURSDAY	FRIDAY	SATURDAY	TASKS

NOTES

MONTHLY PLAN

JAN FEB MAR APR MAY JUN JUL AUG SEP OCT NOV DEC

SUNDAY	MONDAY	TUESDAY	WEDNESDAY
SUNDAY	MONDAY	TUESDAY	WEDNESDAY
SUNDAY	MONDAY	TUESDAY	WEDNESDAY
SUNDAY	MONDAY	TUESDAY	WEDNESDAY
SUNDAY	MONDAY	TUESDAY	WEDNESDAY

NOTES

FOCUS:

THURSDAY	FRIDAY	SATURDAY	TASKS
THURSDAY	FRIDAY	SATURDAY	TASKS
THURSDAY	FRIDAY	SATURDAY	TASKS
THURSDAY	FRIDAY	SATURDAY	TASKS
THURSDAY	FRIDAY	SATURDAY	TASKS

NOTES

NOTES AND BRAINSTORMING

NOTES AND BRAINSTORMING

WEEKLY ACTION PLAN

WEEKLY BATTLE PLAN

WEEK OF _____

BIG WINS

1 _____
2 _____
3 _____

GRATITUDE GIVEN?
☐
☐
☐

GOAL #1

WHY I WANT IT:
WEEKLY OBJECTIVE:
OBSTACLES I AM FACING:
HOW WILL I OVERCOME THEM:
WHO CAN HELP:
TIMEBLOCK ON CALENDAR (DATE/TIME):

GOAL #2

WHY I WANT IT:
WEEKLY OBJECTIVE:
OBSTACLES I AM FACING:
HOW WILL I OVERCOME THEM:
WHO CAN HELP:
TIMEBLOCK ON CALENDAR (DATE/TIME):

GOAL #3

WHY I WANT IT:
WEEKLY OBJECTIVE:
OBSTACLES I AM FACING:
HOW WILL I OVERCOME THEM:
WHO CAN HELP:
TIMEBLOCK ON CALENDAR (DATE/TIME):

MOST IMPORTANT NEXT STEP THIS WEEK:

THINGS I'LL DO TO MAKE THIS WEEK GREAT

PERSONAL	FAMILY/ FRIENDS	RELATIONSHIP	HEALTH

END OF WEEK REVIEW

OBSTACLES	CORE OF THE PROBLEM	BRAINSTORM SOLUTIONS

UNTAPPED OPPORTUNITIES

POTENTIAL REVENUE/NOI	RESOURCES & RISKS	OPPORTUNITY COST

LAST WEEK I LEARNED:

THIS WEEK I WILL LEARN:

DID I ACCOMPLISH MY #1 GOAL? ● YES ● NO

IF YES, CELEBRATE. IF NO, WHY NOT? WHAT'S YOUR PLAN TO GET BACK ON TRACK?

SCHEDULED MEETINGS AND BIG ITEMS FOR THE WEEK

MON

TUE

WED

THU

FRI

SAT

SUN

NOTES

NOTES AND BRAINSTORMING

WEEKLY BATTLE PLAN

WEEK OF _____

BIG WINS   GRATITUDE GIVEN?

1 _____ ☐
2 _____ ☐
3 _____ ☐

GOAL #1

WHY I WANT IT:
WEEKLY OBJECTIVE:
OBSTACLES I AM FACING:
HOW WILL I OVERCOME THEM:
WHO CAN HELP:
TIMEBLOCK ON CALENDAR (DATE/TIME):

GOAL #2

WHY I WANT IT:
WEEKLY OBJECTIVE:
OBSTACLES I AM FACING:
HOW WILL I OVERCOME THEM:
WHO CAN HELP:
TIMEBLOCK ON CALENDAR (DATE/TIME):

GOAL #3

WHY I WANT IT:
WEEKLY OBJECTIVE:
OBSTACLES I AM FACING:
HOW WILL I OVERCOME THEM:
WHO CAN HELP:
TIMEBLOCK ON CALENDAR (DATE/TIME):

MOST IMPORTANT NEXT STEP THIS WEEK:

THINGS I'LL DO TO MAKE THIS WEEK GREAT

PERSONAL	FAMILY/ FRIENDS	RELATIONSHIP	HEALTH

END OF WEEK REVIEW

OBSTACLES	CORE OF THE PROBLEM	BRAINSTORM SOLUTIONS

UNTAPPED OPPORTUNITIES

POTENTIAL REVENUE/NOI	RESOURCES & RISKS	OPPORTUNITY COST

LAST WEEK I LEARNED:

THIS WEEK I WILL LEARN:

DID I ACCOMPLISH MY #1 GOAL?   ● YES   ● NO

IF YES, CELEBRATE. IF NO, WHY NOT? WHAT'S YOUR PLAN TO GET BACK ON TRACK?

SCHEDULED MEETINGS AND BIG ITEMS FOR THE WEEK

MON _____
_____
_____

TUE _____
_____
_____

WED _____
_____
_____

THU _____
_____
_____

FRI _____
_____
_____

SAT _____
_____
_____

SUN _____
_____
_____

NOTES

NOTES AND BRAINSTORMING

WEEKLY BATTLE PLAN

WEEK OF _____

BIG WINS   GRATITUDE GIVEN?

1 _____ ☐
2 _____ ☐
3 _____ ☐

GOAL #1 _____

WHY I WANT IT:
WEEKLY OBJECTIVE:
OBSTACLES I AM FACING:
HOW WILL I OVERCOME THEM:
WHO CAN HELP:
TIMEBLOCK ON CALENDAR (DATE/TIME):

GOAL #2 _____

WHY I WANT IT:
WEEKLY OBJECTIVE:
OBSTACLES I AM FACING:
HOW WILL I OVERCOME THEM:
WHO CAN HELP:
TIMEBLOCK ON CALENDAR (DATE/TIME):

GOAL #3 _____

WHY I WANT IT:
WEEKLY OBJECTIVE:
OBSTACLES I AM FACING:
HOW WILL I OVERCOME THEM:
WHO CAN HELP:
TIMEBLOCK ON CALENDAR (DATE/TIME):

MOST IMPORTANT NEXT STEP THIS WEEK:

THINGS I'LL DO TO MAKE THIS WEEK GREAT

PERSONAL	FAMILY/ FRIENDS	RELATIONSHIP	HEALTH

END OF WEEK REVIEW

OBSTACLES	CORE OF THE PROBLEM	BRAINSTORM SOLUTIONS

UNTAPPED OPPORTUNITIES

POTENTIAL REVENUE/NOI	RESOURCES & RISKS	OPPORTUNITY COST

LAST WEEK I LEARNED:
THIS WEEK I WILL LEARN:
DID I ACCOMPLISH MY #1 GOAL? ● YES ● NO
IF YES, CELEBRATE. IF NO, WHY NOT? WHAT'S YOUR PLAN TO GET BACK ON TRACK?

SCHEDULED MEETINGS AND BIG ITEMS FOR THE WEEK

MON

TUE

WED

THU

FRI

SAT

SUN

NOTES

NOTES AND BRAINSTORMING

DAILY ACTION PLAN

DAILY PLAN

JAN FEB MAR APR MAY JUN JUL AUG SEP OCT NOV DEC
1 2 3 4 5 6 7 8 9 10 11 12 13 14 15 16 17 18 19 20 21 22 23 24 25 26 27 28 29 30 31

MORNING ROUTINE

THREE THINGS I AM GRATEFUL FOR:

_____

_____

_____

THREE THINGS I AM EXCITED FOR:

_____

_____

_____

WOKE UP: _____   HOURS SLEPT: _____   HIT SNOOZE? ■ Y ■ N

FOCUS	TODAY'S PT	REJUVENATE

GOAL #1

WEEKLY OBJECTIVE:
M.I.N.S.:

GOAL #2

WEEKLY OBJECTIVE:
M.I.N.S.:

GOAL #3

WEEKLY OBJECTIVE:
M.I.N.S.:

IF I DO THESE THREE THINGS TODAY I WILL WIN THE DAY!

1. _____
2. _____
3. _____

TIME BLOCKING

0400	1000	1600
0430	1030	1630
0500	1100	1700
0530	1130	1730
0600	1200	1800
0630	1230	1830
0700	1300	1900
0730	1330	1930
0800	1400	2000
0830	1430	2030
0900	1500	2100
0930	1530	2130

SCHEDULE ENOUGH BREAKS? ☐   SCHEDULED M.I.N.S ☐

EVENING REVIEW

DID YOU ACCOMPLISH YOUR M.I.N.S. TODAY?   ☐ YES   ☐ NO

TODAY'S WINS

_____

_____

_____

TODAY I STRUGGLED WITH

_____

_____

_____

OPPORTUNITIES FOR IMPROVEMENT:
SCALE OF 1-10 HOW PRODUCTIVE WERE YOU TODAY?

PLANS FOR TOMORROW:

NOTES

DAILY PLAN

JAN FEB MAR APR MAY JUN JUL AUG SEP OCT NOV DEC
1 2 3 4 5 6 7 8 9 10 11 12 13 14 15 16 17 18 19 20 21 22 23 24 25 26 27 28 29 30 31

MORNING ROUTINE

THREE THINGS I AM GRATEFUL FOR:

_____

_____

_____

THREE THINGS I AM EXCITED FOR:

_____

_____

_____

WOKE UP: _____ HOURS SLEPT: _____ HIT SNOOZE? ■Y ■N

FOCUS	TODAY'S PT	REJUVENATE

GOAL #1
WEEKLY OBJECTIVE:
M.I.N.S.:

GOAL #2
WEEKLY OBJECTIVE:
M.I.N.S.:

GOAL #3
WEEKLY OBJECTIVE:
M.I.N.S.:

IF I DO THESE THREE THINGS TODAY I WILL WIN THE DAY!

1. _____
2. _____
3. _____

TIME BLOCKING

0400	1000	1600
0430	1030	1630
0500	1100	1700
0530	1130	1730
0600	1200	1800
0630	1230	1830
0700	1300	1900
0730	1330	1930
0800	1400	2000
0830	1430	2030
0900	1500	2100
0930	1530	2130

SCHEDULE ENOUGH BREAKS? ☐   SCHEDULED M.I.N.S ☐

EVENING REVIEW

DID YOU ACCOMPLISH YOUR M.I.N.S. TODAY?   ☐ YES   ☐ NO

TODAY'S WINS

_____

_____

_____

TODAY I STRUGGLED WITH

_____

_____

_____

OPPORTUNITIES FOR IMPROVEMENT:
SCALE OF 1-10 HOW PRODUCTIVE WERE YOU TODAY?

PLANS FOR TOMORROW:

NOTES

DAILY PLAN

JAN FEB MAR APR MAY JUN JUL AUG SEP OCT NOV DEC
1 2 3 4 5 6 7 8 9 10 11 12 13 14 15 16 17 18 19 20 21 22 23 24 25 26 27 28 29 30 31

MORNING ROUTINE

THREE THINGS I AM GRATEFUL FOR:

_____

_____

_____

THREE THINGS I AM EXCITED FOR:

_____

_____

_____

WOKE UP: _____ HOURS SLEPT: _____ HIT SNOOZE? ■Y ■N

FOCUS	TODAY'S PT	REJUVENATE

GOAL #1
WEEKLY OBJECTIVE:
M.I.N.S.:

GOAL #2
WEEKLY OBJECTIVE:
M.I.N.S.:

GOAL #3
WEEKLY OBJECTIVE:
M.I.N.S.:

IF I DO THESE THREE THINGS TODAY I WILL WIN THE DAY!

1 _____

2 _____

3 _____

TIME BLOCKING

0400	1000	1600
0430	1030	1630
0500	1100	1700
0530	1130	1730
0600	1200	1800
0630	1230	1830
0700	1300	1900
0730	1330	1930
0800	1400	2000
0830	1430	2030
0900	1500	2100
0930	1530	2130

SCHEDULE ENOUGH BREAKS? ▢   SCHEDULED M.I.N.S ▢

EVENING REVIEW

DID YOU ACCOMPLISH YOUR M.I.N.S. TODAY?   ▢ YES   ▢ NO

TODAY'S WINS

_____

_____

_____

TODAY I STRUGGLED WITH

_____

_____

_____

OPPORTUNITIES FOR IMPROVEMENT:
SCALE OF 1-10 HOW PRODUCTIVE WERE YOU TODAY?

PLANS FOR TOMORROW:

NOTES

DAILY PLAN

JAN FEB MAR APR MAY JUN JUL AUG SEP OCT NOV DEC
1 2 3 4 5 6 7 8 9 10 11 12 13 14 15 16 17 18 19 20 21 22 23 24 25 26 27 28 29 30 31

MORNING ROUTINE

THREE THINGS I AM GRATEFUL FOR:

_____

_____

_____

THREE THINGS I AM EXCITED FOR:

_____

_____

_____

WOKE UP: _____   HOURS SLEPT: _____   HIT SNOOZE? ■ Y ■ N

FOCUS	TODAY'S PT	REJUVENATE

GOAL #1 _____
WEEKLY OBJECTIVE:
M.I.N.S.:

GOAL #2 _____
WEEKLY OBJECTIVE:
M.I.N.S.:

GOAL #3 _____
WEEKLY OBJECTIVE:
M.I.N.S.:

IF I DO THESE THREE THINGS TODAY I WILL WIN THE DAY!

1 _____

2 _____

3 _____

TIME BLOCKING

0400	1000	1600
0430	1030	1630
0500	1100	1700
0530	1130	1730
0600	1200	1800
0630	1230	1830
0700	1300	1900
0730	1330	1930
0800	1400	2000
0830	1430	2030
0900	1500	2100
0930	1530	2130

SCHEDULE ENOUGH BREAKS? ▢   SCHEDULED M.I.N.S ▢

EVENING REVIEW

DID YOU ACCOMPLISH YOUR M.I.N.S. TODAY?   ▢ YES   ▢ NO

TODAY'S WINS

_____
_____
_____

TODAY I STRUGGLED WITH

_____
_____
_____

OPPORTUNITIES FOR IMPROVEMENT:
SCALE OF 1-10 HOW PRODUCTIVE WERE YOU TODAY?

PLANS FOR TOMORROW:

NOTES

DAILY PLAN

JAN FEB MAR APR MAY JUN JUL AUG SEP OCT NOV DEC
1 2 3 4 5 6 7 8 9 10 11 12 13 14 15 16 17 18 19 20 21 22 23 24 25 26 27 28 29 30 31

MORNING ROUTINE

THREE THINGS I AM GRATEFUL FOR:

_____

_____

_____

THREE THINGS I AM EXCITED FOR:

_____

_____

_____

WOKE UP: _____   HOURS SLEPT: _____   HIT SNOOZE? ☐ Y ☐ N

FOCUS	TODAY'S PT	REJUVENATE

GOAL #1
WEEKLY OBJECTIVE:
M.I.N.S.:

GOAL #2
WEEKLY OBJECTIVE:
M.I.N.S.:

GOAL #3
WEEKLY OBJECTIVE:
M.I.N.S.:

IF I DO THESE THREE THINGS TODAY I WILL WIN THE DAY!

1. _____
2. _____
3. _____

TIME BLOCKING

0400	1000	1600
0430	1030	1630
0500	1100	1700
0530	1130	1730
0600	1200	1800
0630	1230	1830
0700	1300	1900
0730	1330	1930
0800	1400	2000
0830	1430	2030
0900	1500	2100
0930	1530	2130

SCHEDULE ENOUGH BREAKS? ▢   SCHEDULED M.I.N.S ▢

EVENING REVIEW

DID YOU ACCOMPLISH YOUR M.I.N.S. TODAY?   ▢ YES   ▢ NO

TODAY'S WINS

_____

_____

_____

TODAY I STRUGGLED WITH

_____

_____

_____

OPPORTUNITIES FOR IMPROVEMENT:
SCALE OF 1-10 HOW PRODUCTIVE WERE YOU TODAY?

PLANS FOR TOMORROW:

NOTES

DAILY PLAN

JAN FEB MAR APR MAY JUN JUL AUG SEP OCT NOV DEC
1 2 3 4 5 6 7 8 9 10 11 12 13 14 15 16 17 18 19 20 21 22 23 24 25 26 27 28 29 30 31

MORNING ROUTINE

THREE THINGS I AM GRATEFUL FOR:

_____

_____

_____

THREE THINGS I AM EXCITED FOR:

_____

_____

_____

WOKE UP: _____   HOURS SLEPT: _____   HIT SNOOZE? ● Y ● N

FOCUS	TODAY'S PT	REJUVENATE

GOAL #1
WEEKLY OBJECTIVE:
M.I.N.S.:

GOAL #2
WEEKLY OBJECTIVE:
M.I.N.S.:

GOAL #3
WEEKLY OBJECTIVE:
M.I.N.S.:

IF I DO THESE THREE THINGS TODAY I WILL WIN THE DAY!

1 _____

2 _____

3 _____

TIME BLOCKING

0400 _____	1000 _____	1600 _____
0430 _____	1030 _____	1630 _____
0500 _____	1100 _____	1700 _____
0530 _____	1130 _____	1730 _____
0600 _____	1200 _____	1800 _____
0630 _____	1230 _____	1830 _____
0700 _____	1300 _____	1900 _____
0730 _____	1330 _____	1930 _____
0800 _____	1400 _____	2000 _____
0830 _____	1430 _____	2030 _____
0900 _____	1500 _____	2100 _____
0930 _____	1530 _____	2130 _____

SCHEDULE ENOUGH BREAKS? ☐   SCHEDULED M.I.N.S ☐

EVENING REVIEW

DID YOU ACCOMPLISH YOUR M.I.N.S. TODAY?   ☐ YES   ☐ NO

TODAY'S WINS

_____

_____

_____

TODAY I STRUGGLED WITH

_____

_____

_____

OPPORTUNITIES FOR IMPROVEMENT:
SCALE OF 1-10 HOW PRODUCTIVE WERE YOU TODAY?

PLANS FOR TOMORROW:

NOTES

DAILY PLAN

JAN FEB MAR APR MAY JUN JUL AUG SEP OCT NOV DEC
1 2 3 4 5 6 7 8 9 10 11 12 13 14 15 16 17 18 19 20 21 22 23 24 25 26 27 28 29 30 31

MORNING ROUTINE

THREE THINGS I AM
GRATEFUL FOR:

_____

_____

_____

THREE THINGS I AM
EXCITED FOR:

_____

_____

_____

WOKE UP: _____   HOURS SLEPT: _____   HIT SNOOZE? ■ Y ■ N

FOCUS	TODAY'S PT	REJUVENATE

GOAL #1
WEEKLY OBJECTIVE:
M.I.N.S.:

GOAL #2
WEEKLY OBJECTIVE:
M.I.N.S.:

GOAL #3
WEEKLY OBJECTIVE:
M.I.N.S.:

IF I DO THESE THREE THINGS TODAY I WILL WIN THE DAY!

1 _____

2 _____

3 _____

TIME BLOCKING

0400	1000	1600
0430	1030	1630
0500	1100	1700
0530	1130	1730
0600	1200	1800
0630	1230	1830
0700	1300	1900
0730	1330	1930
0800	1400	2000
0830	1430	2030
0900	1500	2100
0930	1530	2130

SCHEDULE ENOUGH BREAKS? ☐   SCHEDULED M.I.N.S ☐

EVENING REVIEW

DID YOU ACCOMPLISH YOUR M.I.N.S. TODAY?   ☐ YES   ☐ NO

TODAY'S WINS   **TODAY I STRUGGLED WITH**

_____   _____

_____   _____

_____   _____

OPPORTUNITIES FOR IMPROVEMENT:
SCALE OF 1-10 HOW PRODUCTIVE WERE YOU TODAY?

PLANS FOR TOMORROW: **NOTES**

DAILY PLAN

JAN FEB MAR APR MAY JUN JUL AUG SEP OCT NOV DEC
1 2 3 4 5 6 7 8 9 10 11 12 13 14 15 16 17 18 19 20 21 22 23 24 25 26 27 28 29 30 31

MORNING ROUTINE

THREE THINGS I AM GRATEFUL FOR:

_____

_____

_____

THREE THINGS I AM EXCITED FOR:

_____

_____

_____

WOKE UP: _____   HOURS SLEPT: _____   HIT SNOOZE? ☐ Y ☐ N

FOCUS	TODAY'S PT	REJUVENATE

GOAL #1 _____
WEEKLY OBJECTIVE:
M.I.N.S.:

GOAL #2 _____
WEEKLY OBJECTIVE:
M.I.N.S.:

GOAL #3 _____
WEEKLY OBJECTIVE:
M.I.N.S.:

IF I DO THESE THREE THINGS TODAY I WILL WIN THE DAY!

1 _____

2 _____

3 _____

TIME BLOCKING

0400 _____	1000 _____	1600 _____
0430 _____	1030 _____	1630 _____
0500 _____	1100 _____	1700 _____
0530 _____	1130 _____	1730 _____
0600 _____	1200 _____	1800 _____
0630 _____	1230 _____	1830 _____
0700 _____	1300 _____	1900 _____
0730 _____	1330 _____	1930 _____
0800 _____	1400 _____	2000 _____
0830 _____	1430 _____	2030 _____
0900 _____	1500 _____	2100 _____
0930 _____	1530 _____	2130 _____

SCHEDULE ENOUGH BREAKS? ☐   SCHEDULED M.I.N.S ☐

EVENING REVIEW

DID YOU ACCOMPLISH YOUR M.I.N.S. TODAY?   ☐ YES   ☐ NO

TODAY'S WINS

_____

_____

_____

TODAY I STRUGGLED WITH

_____

_____

_____

OPPORTUNITIES FOR IMPROVEMENT:
SCALE OF 1-10 HOW PRODUCTIVE WERE YOU TODAY?

PLANS FOR TOMORROW:

NOTES

DAILY PLAN

JAN FEB MAR APR MAY JUN JUL AUG SEP OCT NOV DEC
1 2 3 4 5 6 7 8 9 10 11 12 13 14 15 16 17 18 19 20 21 22 23 24 25 26 27 28 29 30 31

MORNING ROUTINE

THREE THINGS I AM GRATEFUL FOR:

_____

_____

_____

THREE THINGS I AM EXCITED FOR:

_____

_____

_____

WOKE UP: _____   HOURS SLEPT: _____   HIT SNOOZE? ☐ Y ☐ N

FOCUS	TODAY'S PT	REJUVENATE

GOAL #1
WEEKLY OBJECTIVE:
M.I.N.S.:

GOAL #2
WEEKLY OBJECTIVE:
M.I.N.S.:

GOAL #3
WEEKLY OBJECTIVE:
M.I.N.S.:

IF I DO THESE THREE THINGS TODAY I WILL WIN THE DAY!

1. _____
2. _____
3. _____

TIME BLOCKING

0400 _____	1000 _____	1600 _____
0430 _____	1030 _____	1630 _____
0500 _____	1100 _____	1700 _____
0530 _____	1130 _____	1730 _____
0600 _____	1200 _____	1800 _____
0630 _____	1230 _____	1830 _____
0700 _____	1300 _____	1900 _____
0730 _____	1330 _____	1930 _____
0800 _____	1400 _____	2000 _____
0830 _____	1430 _____	2030 _____
0900 _____	1500 _____	2100 _____
0930 _____	1530 _____	2130 _____

SCHEDULE ENOUGH BREAKS? ☐   SCHEDULED M.I.N.S ☐

EVENING REVIEW

DID YOU ACCOMPLISH YOUR M.I.N.S. TODAY?   ☐ YES   ☐ NO

TODAY'S WINS

_____

_____

_____

TODAY I STRUGGLED WITH

_____

_____

_____

OPPORTUNITIES FOR IMPROVEMENT:
SCALE OF 1-10 HOW PRODUCTIVE WERE YOU TODAY?

PLANS FOR TOMORROW:

NOTES

DAILY PLAN

JAN FEB MAR APR MAY JUN JUL AUG SEP OCT NOV DEC
1 2 3 4 5 6 7 8 9 10 11 12 13 14 15 16 17 18 19 20 21 22 23 24 25 26 27 28 29 30 31

MORNING ROUTINE

THREE THINGS I AM GRATEFUL FOR:

_____

_____

_____

THREE THINGS I AM EXCITED FOR:

_____

_____

_____

WOKE UP: _____   HOURS SLEPT: _____   HIT SNOOZE? ▪Y ▪N

FOCUS	TODAY'S PT	REJUVENATE

GOAL #1 _____
WEEKLY OBJECTIVE:
M.I.N.S.:

GOAL #2 _____
WEEKLY OBJECTIVE:
M.I.N.S.:

GOAL #3 _____
WEEKLY OBJECTIVE:
M.I.N.S.:

IF I DO THESE THREE THINGS TODAY I WILL WIN THE DAY!

1 _____

2 _____

3 _____

TIME BLOCKING

0400	1000	1600
0430	1030	1630
0500	1100	1700
0530	1130	1730
0600	1200	1800
0630	1230	1830
0700	1300	1900
0730	1330	1930
0800	1400	2000
0830	1430	2030
0900	1500	2100
0930	1530	2130

SCHEDULE ENOUGH BREAKS? ☐   SCHEDULED M.I.N.S ☐

EVENING REVIEW

DID YOU ACCOMPLISH YOUR M.I.N.S. TODAY?   ☐ YES   ☐ NO

TODAY'S WINS

_____

_____

_____

TODAY I STRUGGLED WITH

_____

_____

_____

OPPORTUNITIES FOR IMPROVEMENT:
SCALE OF 1-10 HOW PRODUCTIVE WERE YOU TODAY?

PLANS FOR TOMORROW:

NOTES

DAILY PLAN

JAN FEB MAR APR MAY JUN JUL AUG SEP OCT NOV DEC
1 2 3 4 5 6 7 8 9 10 11 12 13 14 15 16 17 18 19 20 21 22 23 24 25 26 27 28 29 30 31

MORNING ROUTINE

THREE THINGS I AM GRATEFUL FOR:

_____

_____

_____

THREE THINGS I AM EXCITED FOR:

_____

_____

_____

WOKE UP: _____   HOURS SLEPT: _____   HIT SNOOZE? ▪Y ▪N

FOCUS	TODAY'S PT	REJUVENATE

GOAL #1
WEEKLY OBJECTIVE:
M.I.N.S.:

GOAL #2
WEEKLY OBJECTIVE:
M.I.N.S.:

GOAL #3
WEEKLY OBJECTIVE:
M.I.N.S.:

IF I DO THESE THREE THINGS TODAY I WILL WIN THE DAY!

1 _____

2 _____

3 _____

TIME BLOCKING

0400	1000	1600
0430	1030	1630
0500	1100	1700
0530	1130	1730
0600	1200	1800
0630	1230	1830
0700	1300	1900
0730	1330	1930
0800	1400	2000
0830	1430	2030
0900	1500	2100
0930	1530	2130

SCHEDULE ENOUGH BREAKS? ▢   SCHEDULED M.I.N.S ▢

EVENING REVIEW

DID YOU ACCOMPLISH YOUR M.I.N.S. TODAY?   ▢ YES   ▢ NO

TODAY'S WINS

_____

_____

_____

TODAY I STRUGGLED WITH

_____

_____

_____

OPPORTUNITIES FOR IMPROVEMENT:
SCALE OF 1-10 HOW PRODUCTIVE WERE YOU TODAY?

PLANS FOR TOMORROW:

NOTES

DAILY PLAN

JAN FEB MAR APR MAY JUN JUL AUG SEP OCT NOV DEC
1 2 3 4 5 6 7 8 9 10 11 12 13 14 15 16 17 18 19 20 21 22 23 24 25 26 27 28 29 30 31

MORNING ROUTINE

THREE THINGS I AM GRATEFUL FOR:

_____

_____

_____

THREE THINGS I AM EXCITED FOR:

_____

_____

_____

WOKE UP: _____   HOURS SLEPT: _____   HIT SNOOZE? ■Y ■N

FOCUS	TODAY'S PT	REJUVENATE

GOAL #1
WEEKLY OBJECTIVE:
M.I.N.S.:

GOAL #2
WEEKLY OBJECTIVE:
M.I.N.S.:

GOAL #3
WEEKLY OBJECTIVE:
M.I.N.S.:

IF I DO THESE THREE THINGS TODAY I WILL WIN THE DAY!

1 _____

2 _____

3 _____

TIME BLOCKING

0400 _____	1000 _____	1600 _____
0430 _____	1030 _____	1630 _____
0500 _____	1100 _____	1700 _____
0530 _____	1130 _____	1730 _____
0600 _____	1200 _____	1800 _____
0630 _____	1230 _____	1830 _____
0700 _____	1300 _____	1900 _____
0730 _____	1330 _____	1930 _____
0800 _____	1400 _____	2000 _____
0830 _____	1430 _____	2030 _____
0900 _____	1500 _____	2100 _____
0930 _____	1530 _____	2130 _____

SCHEDULE ENOUGH BREAKS? ☐   SCHEDULED M.I.N.S ☐

EVENING REVIEW

DID YOU ACCOMPLISH YOUR M.I.N.S. TODAY?   ☐ YES   ☐ NO

TODAY'S WINS

_____

_____

_____

TODAY I STRUGGLED WITH

_____

_____

_____

OPPORTUNITIES FOR IMPROVEMENT:
SCALE OF 1-10 HOW PRODUCTIVE WERE YOU TODAY?

PLANS FOR TOMORROW:

NOTES

DAILY PLAN

JAN FEB MAR APR MAY JUN JUL AUG SEP OCT NOV DEC
1 2 3 4 5 6 7 8 9 10 11 12 13 14 15 16 17 18 19 20 21 22 23 24 25 26 27 28 29 30 31

MORNING ROUTINE

THREE THINGS I AM GRATEFUL FOR:

_____

_____

_____

THREE THINGS I AM EXCITED FOR:

_____

_____

_____

WOKE UP: _____ HOURS SLEPT: _____ HIT SNOOZE? ☐ Y ☐ N

FOCUS	TODAY'S PT	REJUVENATE

GOAL #1 _____
WEEKLY OBJECTIVE:
M.I.N.S.:

GOAL #2 _____
WEEKLY OBJECTIVE:
M.I.N.S.:

GOAL #3 _____
WEEKLY OBJECTIVE:
M.I.N.S.:

IF I DO THESE THREE THINGS TODAY I WILL WIN THE DAY!

1 _____

2 _____

3 _____

TIME BLOCKING

0400	1000	1600
0430	1030	1630
0500	1100	1700
0530	1130	1730
0600	1200	1800
0630	1230	1830
0700	1300	1900
0730	1330	1930
0800	1400	2000
0830	1430	2030
0900	1500	2100
0930	1530	2130

SCHEDULE ENOUGH BREAKS? ☐   SCHEDULED M.I.N.S ☐

EVENING REVIEW

DID YOU ACCOMPLISH YOUR M.I.N.S. TODAY?   ☐ YES   ☐ NO

TODAY'S WINS

_____

_____

_____

TODAY I STRUGGLED WITH

_____

_____

_____

OPPORTUNITIES FOR IMPROVEMENT:
SCALE OF 1-10 HOW PRODUCTIVE WERE YOU TODAY?

PLANS FOR TOMORROW:

NOTES

DAILY PLAN

JAN FEB MAR APR MAY JUN JUL AUG SEP OCT NOV DEC
1 2 3 4 5 6 7 8 9 10 11 12 13 14 15 16 17 18 19 20 21 22 23 24 25 26 27 28 29 30 31

MORNING ROUTINE

THREE THINGS I AM GRATEFUL FOR:

_____

_____

_____

THREE THINGS I AM EXCITED FOR:

_____

_____

_____

WOKE UP: _____   HOURS SLEPT: _____   HIT SNOOZE? ■Y ■N

FOCUS	TODAY'S PT	REJUVENATE

GOAL #1
WEEKLY OBJECTIVE:
M.I.N.S.:

GOAL #2
WEEKLY OBJECTIVE:
M.I.N.S.:

GOAL #3
WEEKLY OBJECTIVE:
M.I.N.S.:

IF I DO THESE THREE THINGS TODAY I WILL WIN THE DAY!

1. _____
2. _____
3. _____

TIME BLOCKING

0400 _____	1000 _____	1600 _____
0430 _____	1030 _____	1630 _____
0500 _____	1100 _____	1700 _____
0530 _____	1130 _____	1730 _____
0600 _____	1200 _____	1800 _____
0630 _____	1230 _____	1830 _____
0700 _____	1300 _____	1900 _____
0730 _____	1330 _____	1930 _____
0800 _____	1400 _____	2000 _____
0830 _____	1430 _____	2030 _____
0900 _____	1500 _____	2100 _____
0930 _____	1530 _____	2130 _____

SCHEDULE ENOUGH BREAKS? ☐   SCHEDULED M.I.N.S ☐

EVENING REVIEW

DID YOU ACCOMPLISH YOUR M.I.N.S. TODAY?   ☐ YES   ☐ NO

TODAY'S WINS

_____

_____

_____

TODAY I STRUGGLED WITH

_____

_____

_____

OPPORTUNITIES FOR IMPROVEMENT:
SCALE OF 1-10 HOW PRODUCTIVE WERE YOU TODAY?

PLANS FOR TOMORROW:

NOTES

DAILY PLAN

JAN FEB MAR APR MAY JUN JUL AUG SEP OCT NOV DEC
1 2 3 4 5 6 7 8 9 10 11 12 13 14 15 16 17 18 19 20 21 22 23 24 25 26 27 28 29 30 31

MORNING ROUTINE

THREE THINGS I AM GRATEFUL FOR:

_____

_____

_____

THREE THINGS I AM EXCITED FOR:

_____

_____

_____

WOKE UP: _____   HOURS SLEPT: _____   HIT SNOOZE? ■ Y ■ N

FOCUS	TODAY'S PT	REJUVENATE

GOAL #1
WEEKLY OBJECTIVE:
M.I.N.S.:

GOAL #2
WEEKLY OBJECTIVE:
M.I.N.S.:

GOAL #3
WEEKLY OBJECTIVE:
M.I.N.S.:

IF I DO THESE THREE THINGS TODAY I WILL WIN THE DAY!

1 _____

2 _____

3 _____

TIME BLOCKING

0400	1000	1600
0430	1030	1630
0500	1100	1700
0530	1130	1730
0600	1200	1800
0630	1230	1830
0700	1300	1900
0730	1330	1930
0800	1400	2000
0830	1430	2030
0900	1500	2100
0930	1530	2130

SCHEDULE ENOUGH BREAKS? ☐   SCHEDULED M.I.N.S ☐

EVENING REVIEW

DID YOU ACCOMPLISH YOUR M.I.N.S. TODAY?   ☐ YES   ☐ NO

TODAY'S WINS

_____
_____
_____

TODAY I STRUGGLED WITH

_____
_____
_____

OPPORTUNITIES FOR IMPROVEMENT:
SCALE OF 1-10 HOW PRODUCTIVE WERE YOU TODAY?

PLANS FOR TOMORROW:

NOTES

DAILY PLAN

JAN FEB MAR APR MAY JUN JUL AUG SEP OCT NOV DEC
1 2 3 4 5 6 7 8 9 10 11 12 13 14 15 16 17 18 19 20 21 22 23 24 25 26 27 28 29 30 31

MORNING ROUTINE

THREE THINGS I AM
GRATEFUL FOR:

_____

_____

_____

THREE THINGS I AM
EXCITED FOR:

_____

_____

_____

WOKE UP: _____   HOURS SLEPT: _____   HIT SNOOZE? ■Y ■N

FOCUS	TODAY'S PT	REJUVENATE

GOAL #1
WEEKLY OBJECTIVE:
M.I.N.S.:

GOAL #2
WEEKLY OBJECTIVE:
M.I.N.S.:

GOAL #3
WEEKLY OBJECTIVE:
M.I.N.S.:

IF I DO THESE THREE THINGS TODAY I WILL WIN THE DAY!

1 _____

2 _____

3 _____

TIME BLOCKING

0400	1000	1600
0430	1030	1630
0500	1100	1700
0530	1130	1730
0600	1200	1800
0630	1230	1830
0700	1300	1900
0730	1330	1930
0800	1400	2000
0830	1430	2030
0900	1500	2100
0930	1530	2130

SCHEDULE ENOUGH BREAKS? ☐   SCHEDULED M.I.N.S ☐

EVENING REVIEW

DID YOU ACCOMPLISH YOUR M.I.N.S. TODAY?   ☐ YES   ☐ NO

TODAY'S WINS

_____
_____
_____

TODAY I STRUGGLED WITH

_____
_____
_____

OPPORTUNITIES FOR IMPROVEMENT:
SCALE OF 1-10 HOW PRODUCTIVE WERE YOU TODAY?

PLANS FOR TOMORROW:

NOTES

DAILY PLAN

JAN FEB MAR APR MAY JUN JUL AUG SEP OCT NOV DEC
1 2 3 4 5 6 7 8 9 10 11 12 13 14 15 16 17 18 19 20 21 22 23 24 25 26 27 28 29 30 31

MORNING ROUTINE

THREE THINGS I AM GRATEFUL FOR:

_____

_____

_____

THREE THINGS I AM EXCITED FOR:

_____

_____

_____

WOKE UP: _____   HOURS SLEPT: _____   HIT SNOOZE? ■ Y ■ N

FOCUS	TODAY'S PT	REJUVENATE

GOAL #1 _____
WEEKLY OBJECTIVE:
M.I.N.S.:

GOAL #2 _____
WEEKLY OBJECTIVE:
M.I.N.S.:

GOAL #3 _____
WEEKLY OBJECTIVE:
M.I.N.S.:

IF I DO THESE THREE THINGS TODAY I WILL WIN THE DAY!

1 _____

2 _____

3 _____

TIME BLOCKING

0400	1000	1600
0430	1030	1630
0500	1100	1700
0530	1130	1730
0600	1200	1800
0630	1230	1830
0700	1300	1900
0730	1330	1930
0800	1400	2000
0830	1430	2030
0900	1500	2100
0930	1530	2130

SCHEDULE ENOUGH BREAKS?   SCHEDULED M.I.N.S

EVENING REVIEW

DID YOU ACCOMPLISH YOUR M.I.N.S. TODAY?   YES   NO

TODAY'S WINS

TODAY I STRUGGLED WITH

OPPORTUNITIES FOR IMPROVEMENT:
SCALE OF 1-10 HOW PRODUCTIVE WERE YOU TODAY?

PLANS FOR TOMORROW:

NOTES

DAILY PLAN

JAN FEB MAR APR MAY JUN JUL AUG SEP OCT NOV DEC
1 2 3 4 5 6 7 8 9 10 11 12 13 14 15 16 17 18 19 20 21 22 23 24 25 26 27 28 29 30 31

MORNING ROUTINE

THREE THINGS I AM GRATEFUL FOR:

_____

_____

_____

THREE THINGS I AM EXCITED FOR:

_____

_____

_____

WOKE UP: _____   HOURS SLEPT: _____   HIT SNOOZE? ■Y ■N

FOCUS	TODAY'S PT	REJUVENATE

GOAL #1
WEEKLY OBJECTIVE:
M.I.N.S.:

GOAL #2
WEEKLY OBJECTIVE:
M.I.N.S.:

GOAL #3
WEEKLY OBJECTIVE:
M.I.N.S.:

IF I DO THESE THREE THINGS TODAY I WILL WIN THE DAY!

1. _____
2. _____
3. _____

TIME BLOCKING

0400	1000	1600
0430	1030	1630
0500	1100	1700
0530	1130	1730
0600	1200	1800
0630	1230	1830
0700	1300	1900
0730	1330	1930
0800	1400	2000
0830	1430	2030
0900	1500	2100
0930	1530	2130

SCHEDULE ENOUGH BREAKS? ☐   SCHEDULED M.I.N.S ☐

EVENING REVIEW

DID YOU ACCOMPLISH YOUR M.I.N.S. TODAY?   ☐ YES   ☐ NO

TODAY'S WINS

_____

_____

_____

TODAY I STRUGGLED WITH

_____

_____

_____

OPPORTUNITIES FOR IMPROVEMENT:
SCALE OF 1-10 HOW PRODUCTIVE WERE YOU TODAY?

PLANS FOR TOMORROW:

NOTES

DAILY PLAN

JAN FEB MAR APR MAY JUN JUL AUG SEP OCT NOV DEC
1 2 3 4 5 6 7 8 9 10 11 12 13 14 15 16 17 18 19 20 21 22 23 24 25 26 27 28 29 30 31

MORNING ROUTINE

THREE THINGS I AM GRATEFUL FOR:

_____

_____

_____

THREE THINGS I AM EXCITED FOR:

_____

_____

_____

WOKE UP: _____   HOURS SLEPT: _____   HIT SNOOZE? ■Y ■N

FOCUS	TODAY'S PT	REJUVENATE

GOAL #1
WEEKLY OBJECTIVE:
M.I.N.S.:

GOAL #2
WEEKLY OBJECTIVE:
M.I.N.S.:

GOAL #3
WEEKLY OBJECTIVE:
M.I.N.S.:

IF I DO THESE THREE THINGS TODAY I WILL WIN THE DAY!

1 _____

2 _____

3 _____

TIME BLOCKING

0400	1000	1600
0430	1030	1630
0500	1100	1700
0530	1130	1730
0600	1200	1800
0630	1230	1830
0700	1300	1900
0730	1330	1930
0800	1400	2000
0830	1430	2030
0900	1500	2100
0930	1530	2130

SCHEDULE ENOUGH BREAKS? ☐   SCHEDULED M.I.N.S ☐

EVENING REVIEW

DID YOU ACCOMPLISH YOUR M.I.N.S. TODAY?   ☐ YES   ☐ NO

TODAY'S WINS

_____

_____

_____

TODAY I STRUGGLED WITH

_____

_____

_____

OPPORTUNITIES FOR IMPROVEMENT:
SCALE OF 1-10 HOW PRODUCTIVE WERE YOU TODAY?

PLANS FOR TOMORROW:

NOTES

DAILY PLAN

JAN FEB MAR APR MAY JUN JUL AUG SEP OCT NOV DEC
1 2 3 4 5 6 7 8 9 10 11 12 13 14 15 16 17 18 19 20 21 22 23 24 25 26 27 28 29 30 31

MORNING ROUTINE

THREE THINGS I AM GRATEFUL FOR:

_____

_____

_____

THREE THINGS I AM EXCITED FOR:

_____

_____

_____

WOKE UP: _____   HOURS SLEPT: _____   HIT SNOOZE? ☐ Y ☐ N

FOCUS	TODAY'S PT	REJUVENATE

GOAL #1
WEEKLY OBJECTIVE:
M.I.N.S.:

GOAL #2
WEEKLY OBJECTIVE:
M.I.N.S.:

GOAL #3
WEEKLY OBJECTIVE:
M.I.N.S.:

IF I DO THESE THREE THINGS TODAY I WILL WIN THE DAY!

1. _____
2. _____
3. _____

TIME BLOCKING

0400	1000	1600
0430	1030	1630
0500	1100	1700
0530	1130	1730
0600	1200	1800
0630	1230	1830
0700	1300	1900
0730	1330	1930
0800	1400	2000
0830	1430	2030
0900	1500	2100
0930	1530	2130

SCHEDULE ENOUGH BREAKS? ☐   SCHEDULED M.I.N.S ☐

EVENING REVIEW

DID YOU ACCOMPLISH YOUR M.I.N.S. TODAY? ☐ YES ☐ NO

TODAY'S WINS

_____
_____
_____

TODAY I STRUGGLED WITH

_____
_____
_____

OPPORTUNITIES FOR IMPROVEMENT:
SCALE OF 1-10 HOW PRODUCTIVE WERE YOU TODAY?

PLANS FOR TOMORROW:

NOTES

DAILY PLAN

JAN FEB MAR APR MAY JUN JUL AUG SEP OCT NOV DEC
1 2 3 4 5 6 7 8 9 10 11 12 13 14 15 16 17 18 19 20 21 22 23 24 25 26 27 28 29 30 31

MORNING ROUTINE

THREE THINGS I AM GRATEFUL FOR:

_____

_____

_____

THREE THINGS I AM EXCITED FOR:

_____

_____

_____

WOKE UP: _____   HOURS SLEPT: _____   HIT SNOOZE? ▪Y ▪N

FOCUS	TODAY'S PT	REJUVENATE

GOAL #1 _____
WEEKLY OBJECTIVE:
M.I.N.S.:

GOAL #2 _____
WEEKLY OBJECTIVE:
M.I.N.S.:

GOAL #3 _____
WEEKLY OBJECTIVE:
M.I.N.S.:

IF I DO THESE THREE THINGS TODAY I WILL WIN THE DAY!

1 _____

2 _____

3 _____

TIME BLOCKING

0400	1000	1600
0430	1030	1630
0500	1100	1700
0530	1130	1730
0600	1200	1800
0630	1230	1830
0700	1300	1900
0730	1330	1930
0800	1400	2000
0830	1430	2030
0900	1500	2100
0930	1530	2130

SCHEDULE ENOUGH BREAKS? ☐   SCHEDULED M.I.N.S ☐

EVENING REVIEW

DID YOU ACCOMPLISH YOUR M.I.N.S. TODAY?   ☐ YES   ☐ NO

TODAY'S WINS

_____

_____

_____

TODAY I STRUGGLED WITH

_____

_____

_____

OPPORTUNITIES FOR IMPROVEMENT:
SCALE OF 1-10 HOW PRODUCTIVE WERE YOU TODAY?

PLANS FOR TOMORROW:

NOTES

DAILY PLAN

JAN FEB MAR APR MAY JUN JUL AUG SEP OCT NOV DEC
1 2 3 4 5 6 7 8 9 10 11 12 13 14 15 16 17 18 19 20 21 22 23 24 25 26 27 28 29 30 31

MORNING ROUTINE

THREE THINGS I AM GRATEFUL FOR:

_____

_____

_____

THREE THINGS I AM EXCITED FOR:

_____

_____

_____

WOKE UP: _____   HOURS SLEPT: _____   HIT SNOOZE? ▪Y ▪N

FOCUS	TODAY'S PT	REJUVENATE

GOAL #1
WEEKLY OBJECTIVE:
M.I.N.S.:

GOAL #2
WEEKLY OBJECTIVE:
M.I.N.S.:

GOAL #3
WEEKLY OBJECTIVE:
M.I.N.S.:

IF I DO THESE THREE THINGS TODAY I WILL WIN THE DAY!

1 _____

2 _____

3 _____

TIME BLOCKING

0400	1000	1600
0430	1030	1630
0500	1100	1700
0530	1130	1730
0600	1200	1800
0630	1230	1830
0700	1300	1900
0730	1330	1930
0800	1400	2000
0830	1430	2030
0900	1500	2100
0930	1530	2130

SCHEDULE ENOUGH BREAKS? ☐   SCHEDULED M.I.N.S ☐

EVENING REVIEW

DID YOU ACCOMPLISH YOUR M.I.N.S. TODAY?   ☐ YES   ☐ NO

TODAY'S WINS

_____

_____

_____

TODAY I STRUGGLED WITH

_____

_____

_____

OPPORTUNITIES FOR IMPROVEMENT:
SCALE OF 1-10 HOW PRODUCTIVE WERE YOU TODAY?

PLANS FOR TOMORROW:

NOTES

DAILY PLAN

JAN FEB MAR APR MAY JUN JUL AUG SEP OCT NOV DEC
1 2 3 4 5 6 7 8 9 10 11 12 13 14 15 16 17 18 19 20 21 22 23 24 25 26 27 28 29 30 31

MORNING ROUTINE

THREE THINGS I AM GRATEFUL FOR:

_____

_____

_____

THREE THINGS I AM EXCITED FOR:

_____

_____

_____

WOKE UP: _____ HOURS SLEPT: _____ HIT SNOOZE? ☐ Y ☐ N

FOCUS	TODAY'S PT	REJUVENATE

GOAL #1
WEEKLY OBJECTIVE:
M.I.N.S.:

GOAL #2
WEEKLY OBJECTIVE:
M.I.N.S.:

GOAL #3
WEEKLY OBJECTIVE:
M.I.N.S.:

IF I DO THESE THREE THINGS TODAY I WILL WIN THE DAY!

1 _____

2 _____

3 _____

TIME BLOCKING

0400	1000	1600
0430	1030	1630
0500	1100	1700
0530	1130	1730
0600	1200	1800
0630	1230	1830
0700	1300	1900
0730	1330	1930
0800	1400	2000
0830	1430	2030
0900	1500	2100
0930	1530	2130

SCHEDULE ENOUGH BREAKS? ☐   SCHEDULED M.I.N.S ☐

EVENING REVIEW

DID YOU ACCOMPLISH YOUR M.I.N.S. TODAY?   ☐ YES   ☐ NO

TODAY'S WINS

_____

_____

_____

TODAY I STRUGGLED WITH

_____

_____

_____

OPPORTUNITIES FOR IMPROVEMENT:
SCALE OF 1-10 HOW PRODUCTIVE WERE YOU TODAY?

PLANS FOR TOMORROW:

NOTES

DAILY PLAN

JAN FEB MAR APR MAY JUN JUL AUG SEP OCT NOV DEC
1 2 3 4 5 6 7 8 9 10 11 12 13 14 15 16 17 18 19 20 21 22 23 24 25 26 27 28 29 30 31

MORNING ROUTINE

THREE THINGS I AM GRATEFUL FOR:

_____

_____

_____

THREE THINGS I AM EXCITED FOR:

_____

_____

_____

WOKE UP: _____   HOURS SLEPT: _____   HIT SNOOZE? ■Y ■N

FOCUS	TODAY'S PT	REJUVENATE

GOAL #1
WEEKLY OBJECTIVE: _____
M.I.N.S.: _____

GOAL #2
WEEKLY OBJECTIVE: _____
M.I.N.S.: _____

GOAL #3
WEEKLY OBJECTIVE: _____
M.I.N.S.: _____

IF I DO THESE THREE THINGS TODAY I WILL WIN THE DAY!

1 _____

2 _____

3 _____

TIME BLOCKING

0400 _____	1000 _____	1600 _____
0430 _____	1030 _____	1630 _____
0500 _____	1100 _____	1700 _____
0530 _____	1130 _____	1730 _____
0600 _____	1200 _____	1800 _____
0630 _____	1230 _____	1830 _____
0700 _____	1300 _____	1900 _____
0730 _____	1330 _____	1930 _____
0800 _____	1400 _____	2000 _____
0830 _____	1430 _____	2030 _____
0900 _____	1500 _____	2100 _____
0930 _____	1530 _____	2130 _____

SCHEDULE ENOUGH BREAKS? ☐   SCHEDULED M.I.N.S ☐

EVENING REVIEW

DID YOU ACCOMPLISH YOUR M.I.N.S. TODAY?   ☐ YES   ☐ NO

TODAY'S WINS

_____

_____

_____

TODAY I STRUGGLED WITH

_____

_____

_____

OPPORTUNITIES FOR IMPROVEMENT:
SCALE OF 1-10 HOW PRODUCTIVE WERE YOU TODAY?

PLANS FOR TOMORROW:

NOTES

DAILY PLAN

JAN FEB MAR APR MAY JUN JUL AUG SEP OCT NOV DEC
1 2 3 4 5 6 7 8 9 10 11 12 13 14 15 16 17 18 19 20 21 22 23 24 25 26 27 28 29 30 31

MORNING ROUTINE

THREE THINGS I AM GRATEFUL FOR:

_____

_____

_____

THREE THINGS I AM EXCITED FOR:

_____

_____

_____

WOKE UP: _____ HOURS SLEPT: _____ HIT SNOOZE? ■Y ■N

FOCUS	TODAY'S PT	REJUVENATE

GOAL #1 _____
WEEKLY OBJECTIVE:
M.I.N.S.:

GOAL #2 _____
WEEKLY OBJECTIVE:
M.I.N.S.:

GOAL #3 _____
WEEKLY OBJECTIVE:
M.I.N.S.:

IF I DO THESE THREE THINGS TODAY I WILL WIN THE DAY!

1 _____

2 _____

3 _____

TIME BLOCKING

0400	1000	1600
0430	1030	1630
0500	1100	1700
0530	1130	1730
0600	1200	1800
0630	1230	1830
0700	1300	1900
0730	1330	1930
0800	1400	2000
0830	1430	2030
0900	1500	2100
0930	1530	2130

SCHEDULE ENOUGH BREAKS?   SCHEDULED M.I.N.S

EVENING REVIEW

DID YOU ACCOMPLISH YOUR M.I.N.S. TODAY?   YES   NO

TODAY'S WINS

TODAY I STRUGGLED WITH

OPPORTUNITIES FOR IMPROVEMENT:
SCALE OF 1-10 HOW PRODUCTIVE WERE YOU TODAY?

PLANS FOR TOMORROW:

NOTES

DAILY PLAN

JAN FEB MAR APR MAY JUN JUL AUG SEP OCT NOV DEC
1 2 3 4 5 6 7 8 9 10 11 12 13 14 15 16 17 18 19 20 21 22 23 24 25 26 27 28 29 30 31

MORNING ROUTINE

THREE THINGS I AM GRATEFUL FOR:

_____

_____

_____

THREE THINGS I AM EXCITED FOR:

_____

_____

_____

WOKE UP: _____   HOURS SLEPT: _____   HIT SNOOZE? ■ Y ■ N

FOCUS	TODAY'S PT	REJUVENATE

GOAL #1
WEEKLY OBJECTIVE:
M.I.N.S.:

GOAL #2
WEEKLY OBJECTIVE:
M.I.N.S.:

GOAL #3
WEEKLY OBJECTIVE:
M.I.N.S.:

IF I DO THESE THREE THINGS TODAY I WILL WIN THE DAY!

1 _____

2 _____

3 _____

TIME BLOCKING

0400 _____	1000 _____	1600 _____
0430 _____	1030 _____	1630 _____
0500 _____	1100 _____	1700 _____
0530 _____	1130 _____	1730 _____
0600 _____	1200 _____	1800 _____
0630 _____	1230 _____	1830 _____
0700 _____	1300 _____	1900 _____
0730 _____	1330 _____	1930 _____
0800 _____	1400 _____	2000 _____
0830 _____	1430 _____	2030 _____
0900 _____	1500 _____	2100 _____
0930 _____	1530 _____	2130 _____

SCHEDULE ENOUGH BREAKS? ☐   SCHEDULED M.I.N.S ☐

EVENING REVIEW

DID YOU ACCOMPLISH YOUR M.I.N.S. TODAY?   ☐ YES   ☐ NO

TODAY'S WINS

_____

_____

_____

TODAY I STRUGGLED WITH

_____

_____

_____

OPPORTUNITIES FOR IMPROVEMENT:
SCALE OF 1-10 HOW PRODUCTIVE WERE YOU TODAY?

PLANS FOR TOMORROW:

NOTES

DAILY PLAN

JAN FEB MAR APR MAY JUN JUL AUG SEP OCT NOV DEC
1 2 3 4 5 6 7 8 9 10 11 12 13 14 15 16 17 18 19 20 21 22 23 24 25 26 27 28 29 30 31

MORNING ROUTINE

THREE THINGS I AM GRATEFUL FOR:

_____

_____

_____

THREE THINGS I AM EXCITED FOR:

_____

_____

_____

WOKE UP: _____   HOURS SLEPT: _____   HIT SNOOZE? ■ Y ■ N

FOCUS	TODAY'S PT	REJUVENATE

GOAL #1
WEEKLY OBJECTIVE:
M.I.N.S.:

GOAL #2
WEEKLY OBJECTIVE:
M.I.N.S.:

GOAL #3
WEEKLY OBJECTIVE:
M.I.N.S.:

IF I DO THESE THREE THINGS TODAY I WILL WIN THE DAY!

1 _____

2 _____

3 _____

TIME BLOCKING

0400	1000	1600
0430	1030	1630
0500	1100	1700
0530	1130	1730
0600	1200	1800
0630	1230	1830
0700	1300	1900
0730	1330	1930
0800	1400	2000
0830	1430	2030
0900	1500	2100
0930	1530	2130

SCHEDULE ENOUGH BREAKS? ☐   SCHEDULED M.I.N.S ☐

EVENING REVIEW

DID YOU ACCOMPLISH YOUR M.I.N.S. TODAY?   ☐ YES   ☐ NO

TODAY'S WINS

_____

_____

_____

TODAY I STRUGGLED WITH

_____

_____

_____

OPPORTUNITIES FOR IMPROVEMENT:
SCALE OF 1-10 HOW PRODUCTIVE WERE YOU TODAY?

PLANS FOR TOMORROW:

NOTES

DAILY PLAN

JAN FEB MAR APR MAY JUN JUL AUG SEP OCT NOV DEC
1 2 3 4 5 6 7 8 9 10 11 12 13 14 15 16 17 18 19 20 21 22 23 24 25 26 27 28 29 30 31

MORNING ROUTINE

THREE THINGS I AM GRATEFUL FOR:

_____

_____

_____

THREE THINGS I AM EXCITED FOR:

_____

_____

_____

WOKE UP: _____   HOURS SLEPT: _____   HIT SNOOZE? ■Y ■N

FOCUS	TODAY'S PT	REJUVENATE

GOAL #1 _____
WEEKLY OBJECTIVE:
M.I.N.S.:

GOAL #2 _____
WEEKLY OBJECTIVE:
M.I.N.S.:

GOAL #3 _____
WEEKLY OBJECTIVE:
M.I.N.S.:

IF I DO THESE THREE THINGS TODAY I WILL WIN THE DAY!

1. _____
2. _____
3. _____

TIME BLOCKING

0400	1000	1600
0430	1030	1630
0500	1100	1700
0530	1130	1730
0600	1200	1800
0630	1230	1830
0700	1300	1900
0730	1330	1930
0800	1400	2000
0830	1430	2030
0900	1500	2100
0930	1530	2130

SCHEDULE ENOUGH BREAKS?   SCHEDULED M.I.N.S

EVENING REVIEW

DID YOU ACCOMPLISH YOUR M.I.N.S. TODAY?   YES   NO

TODAY'S WINS

TODAY I STRUGGLED WITH

_____   _____

_____   _____

_____   _____

OPPORTUNITIES FOR IMPROVEMENT:
SCALE OF 1-10 HOW PRODUCTIVE WERE YOU TODAY?

PLANS FOR TOMORROW:

NOTES

DAILY PLAN

JAN FEB MAR APR MAY JUN JUL AUG SEP OCT NOV DEC
1 2 3 4 5 6 7 8 9 10 11 12 13 14 15 16 17 18 19 20 21 22 23 24 25 26 27 28 29 30 31

MORNING ROUTINE

THREE THINGS I AM GRATEFUL FOR:

_____

_____

_____

THREE THINGS I AM EXCITED FOR:

_____

_____

_____

WOKE UP: _____   HOURS SLEPT: _____   HIT SNOOZE? ■ Y ■ N

FOCUS	TODAY'S PT	REJUVENATE

GOAL #1
WEEKLY OBJECTIVE:
M.I.N.S.:

GOAL #2
WEEKLY OBJECTIVE:
M.I.N.S.:

GOAL #3
WEEKLY OBJECTIVE:
M.I.N.S.:

IF I DO THESE THREE THINGS TODAY I WILL WIN THE DAY!

1 _____

2 _____

3 _____

TIME BLOCKING

0400 _____	1000 _____	1600 _____
0430 _____	1030 _____	1630 _____
0500 _____	1100 _____	1700 _____
0530 _____	1130 _____	1730 _____
0600 _____	1200 _____	1800 _____
0630 _____	1230 _____	1830 _____
0700 _____	1300 _____	1900 _____
0730 _____	1330 _____	1930 _____
0800 _____	1400 _____	2000 _____
0830 _____	1430 _____	2030 _____
0900 _____	1500 _____	2100 _____
0930 _____	1530 _____	2130 _____

SCHEDULE ENOUGH BREAKS? ☐   SCHEDULED M.I.N.S ☐

EVENING REVIEW

DID YOU ACCOMPLISH YOUR M.I.N.S. TODAY?   ☐ YES   ☐ NO

TODAY'S WINS

_____

_____

_____

TODAY I STRUGGLED WITH

_____

_____

_____

OPPORTUNITIES FOR IMPROVEMENT:
SCALE OF 1-10 HOW PRODUCTIVE WERE YOU TODAY?

PLANS FOR TOMORROW:

NOTES

DAILY PLAN

JAN FEB MAR APR MAY JUN JUL AUG SEP OCT NOV DEC
1 2 3 4 5 6 7 8 9 10 11 12 13 14 15 16 17 18 19 20 21 22 23 24 25 26 27 28 29 30 31

MORNING ROUTINE

THREE THINGS I AM GRATEFUL FOR:

_____

_____

_____

THREE THINGS I AM EXCITED FOR:

_____

_____

_____

WOKE UP: _____ HOURS SLEPT: _____ HIT SNOOZE? ■Y ■N

FOCUS	TODAY'S PT	REJUVENATE

GOAL #1 _____
WEEKLY OBJECTIVE:
M.I.N.S.:

GOAL #2 _____
WEEKLY OBJECTIVE:
M.I.N.S.:

GOAL #3 _____
WEEKLY OBJECTIVE:
M.I.N.S.:

IF I DO THESE THREE THINGS TODAY I WILL WIN THE DAY!

1 _____

2 _____

3 _____

TIME BLOCKING

0400	1000	1600
0430	1030	1630
0500	1100	1700
0530	1130	1730
0600	1200	1800
0630	1230	1830
0700	1300	1900
0730	1330	1930
0800	1400	2000
0830	1430	2030
0900	1500	2100
0930	1530	2130

SCHEDULE ENOUGH BREAKS? ▪   SCHEDULED M.I.N.S ▪

EVENING REVIEW

DID YOU ACCOMPLISH YOUR M.I.N.S. TODAY?   ▪ YES   ▪ NO

TODAY'S WINS

_____

_____

_____

TODAY I STRUGGLED WITH

_____

_____

_____

OPPORTUNITIES FOR IMPROVEMENT:
SCALE OF 1-10 HOW PRODUCTIVE WERE YOU TODAY?

PLANS FOR TOMORROW:

NOTES

DAILY PLAN

JAN FEB MAR APR MAY JUN JUL AUG SEP OCT NOV DEC
1 2 3 4 5 6 7 8 9 10 11 12 13 14 15 16 17 18 19 20 21 22 23 24 25 26 27 28 29 30 31

MORNING ROUTINE

THREE THINGS I AM GRATEFUL FOR:

_____

_____

_____

THREE THINGS I AM EXCITED FOR:

_____

_____

_____

WOKE UP: _____   HOURS SLEPT: _____   HIT SNOOZE? ☐ Y ☐ N

FOCUS	TODAY'S PT	REJUVENATE

GOAL #1 _____
WEEKLY OBJECTIVE:
M.I.N.S.:

GOAL #2 _____
WEEKLY OBJECTIVE:
M.I.N.S.:

GOAL #3 _____
WEEKLY OBJECTIVE:
M.I.N.S.:

IF I DO THESE THREE THINGS TODAY I WILL WIN THE DAY!

1 _____

2 _____

3 _____

TIME BLOCKING

0400	1000	1600
0430	1030	1630
0500	1100	1700
0530	1130	1730
0600	1200	1800
0630	1230	1830
0700	1300	1900
0730	1330	1930
0800	1400	2000
0830	1430	2030
0900	1500	2100
0930	1530	2130

SCHEDULE ENOUGH BREAKS? ▢   SCHEDULED M.I.N.S ▢

EVENING REVIEW

DID YOU ACCOMPLISH YOUR M.I.N.S. TODAY?   ▢ YES   ▢ NO

TODAY'S WINS

_____

_____

_____

TODAY I STRUGGLED WITH

_____

_____

_____

OPPORTUNITIES FOR IMPROVEMENT:
SCALE OF 1-10 HOW PRODUCTIVE WERE YOU TODAY?

PLANS FOR TOMORROW:

NOTES

DAILY PLAN

JAN FEB MAR APR MAY JUN JUL AUG SEP OCT NOV DEC
1 2 3 4 5 6 7 8 9 10 11 12 13 14 15 16 17 18 19 20 21 22 23 24 25 26 27 28 29 30 31

MORNING ROUTINE

THREE THINGS I AM GRATEFUL FOR:

_____

_____

_____

THREE THINGS I AM EXCITED FOR:

_____

_____

_____

WOKE UP: _____   HOURS SLEPT: _____   HIT SNOOZE? ▪Y ▪N

FOCUS	TODAY'S PT	REJUVENATE

GOAL #1 _____
WEEKLY OBJECTIVE:
M.I.N.S.:

GOAL #2 _____
WEEKLY OBJECTIVE:
M.I.N.S.:

GOAL #3 _____
WEEKLY OBJECTIVE:
M.I.N.S.:

IF I DO THESE THREE THINGS TODAY I WILL WIN THE DAY!

1 _____

2 _____

3 _____

TIME BLOCKING

0400 _____	1000 _____	1600 _____
0430 _____	1030 _____	1630 _____
0500 _____	1100 _____	1700 _____
0530 _____	1130 _____	1730 _____
0600 _____	1200 _____	1800 _____
0630 _____	1230 _____	1830 _____
0700 _____	1300 _____	1900 _____
0730 _____	1330 _____	1930 _____
0800 _____	1400 _____	2000 _____
0830 _____	1430 _____	2030 _____
0900 _____	1500 _____	2100 _____
0930 _____	1530 _____	2130 _____

SCHEDULE ENOUGH BREAKS? ☐   SCHEDULED M.I.N.S ☐

EVENING REVIEW

DID YOU ACCOMPLISH YOUR M.I.N.S. TODAY?   ☐ YES   ☐ NO

TODAY'S WINS

_____

_____

_____

TODAY I STRUGGLED WITH

_____

_____

_____

OPPORTUNITIES FOR IMPROVEMENT:
SCALE OF 1-10 HOW PRODUCTIVE WERE YOU TODAY?

PLANS FOR TOMORROW:

NOTES

DAILY PLAN

JAN FEB MAR APR MAY JUN JUL AUG SEP OCT NOV DEC
1 2 3 4 5 6 7 8 9 10 11 12 13 14 15 16 17 18 19 20 21 22 23 24 25 26 27 28 29 30 31

MORNING ROUTINE

THREE THINGS I AM GRATEFUL FOR:

_____

_____

_____

THREE THINGS I AM EXCITED FOR:

_____

_____

_____

WOKE UP: _____   HOURS SLEPT: _____   HIT SNOOZE? ▪Y ▪N

FOCUS	TODAY'S PT	REJUVENATE

GOAL #1
WEEKLY OBJECTIVE:
M.I.N.S.:

GOAL #2
WEEKLY OBJECTIVE:
M.I.N.S.:

GOAL #3
WEEKLY OBJECTIVE:
M.I.N.S.:

IF I DO THESE THREE THINGS TODAY I WILL WIN THE DAY!

1 _____

2 _____

3 _____

TIME BLOCKING

0400	1000	1600
0430	1030	1630
0500	1100	1700
0530	1130	1730
0600	1200	1800
0630	1230	1830
0700	1300	1900
0730	1330	1930
0800	1400	2000
0830	1430	2030
0900	1500	2100
0930	1530	2130

SCHEDULE ENOUGH BREAKS? ☐   SCHEDULED M.I.N.S ☐

EVENING REVIEW

DID YOU ACCOMPLISH YOUR M.I.N.S. TODAY?   ☐ YES   ☐ NO

TODAY'S WINS

_____

_____

_____

TODAY I STRUGGLED WITH

_____

_____

_____

OPPORTUNITIES FOR IMPROVEMENT:
SCALE OF 1-10 HOW PRODUCTIVE WERE YOU TODAY?

PLANS FOR TOMORROW:

NOTES

DAILY PLAN

JAN FEB MAR APR MAY JUN JUL AUG SEP OCT NOV DEC
1 2 3 4 5 6 7 8 9 10 11 12 13 14 15 16 17 18 19 20 21 22 23 24 25 26 27 28 29 30 31

MORNING ROUTINE

THREE THINGS I AM GRATEFUL FOR:

_____

_____

_____

THREE THINGS I AM EXCITED FOR:

_____

_____

_____

WOKE UP: ☐   HOURS SLEPT: ☐   HIT SNOOZE? ☐ Y ☐ N

FOCUS	TODAY'S PT	REJUVENATE

GOAL #1 _____
WEEKLY OBJECTIVE:
M.I.N.S.:

GOAL #2 _____
WEEKLY OBJECTIVE:
M.I.N.S.:

GOAL #3 _____
WEEKLY OBJECTIVE:
M.I.N.S.:

IF I DO THESE THREE THINGS TODAY I WILL WIN THE DAY!

1. _____

2. _____

3. _____

TIME BLOCKING

0400	1000	1600
0430	1030	1630
0500	1100	1700
0530	1130	1730
0600	1200	1800
0630	1230	1830
0700	1300	1900
0730	1330	1930
0800	1400	2000
0830	1430	2030
0900	1500	2100
0930	1530	2130

SCHEDULE ENOUGH BREAKS? ☐ SCHEDULED M.I.N.S ☐

EVENING REVIEW

DID YOU ACCOMPLISH YOUR M.I.N.S. TODAY? ☐ YES ☐ NO

TODAY'S WINS

___

___

___

TODAY I STRUGGLED WITH

___

___

___

OPPORTUNITIES FOR IMPROVEMENT:

SCALE OF 1-10 HOW PRODUCTIVE WERE YOU TODAY?

PLANS FOR TOMORROW:

NOTES

DAILY PLAN

JAN   FEB   MAR   APR   MAY   JUN   JUL   AUG   SEP   OCT   NOV   DEC
1 2 3 4 5 6 7 8 9 10 11 12 13 14 15 16 17 18 19 20 21 22 23 24 25 26 27 28 29 30 31

MORNING ROUTINE

THREE THINGS I AM GRATEFUL FOR:

_____

_____

_____

THREE THINGS I AM EXCITED FOR:

_____

_____

_____

WOKE UP: _____   HOURS SLEPT: _____   HIT SNOOZE? ▪Y ▪N

| FOCUS | TODAY'S PT | REJUVENATE |

GOAL #1
WEEKLY OBJECTIVE:
M.I.N.S.:

GOAL #2
WEEKLY OBJECTIVE:
M.I.N.S.:

GOAL #3
WEEKLY OBJECTIVE:
M.I.N.S.:

IF I DO THESE THREE THINGS TODAY I WILL WIN THE DAY!

1 _____

2 _____

3 _____

TIME BLOCKING

0400 _____	1000 _____	1600 _____
0430 _____	1030 _____	1630 _____
0500 _____	1100 _____	1700 _____
0530 _____	1130 _____	1730 _____
0600 _____	1200 _____	1800 _____
0630 _____	1230 _____	1830 _____
0700 _____	1300 _____	1900 _____
0730 _____	1330 _____	1930 _____
0800 _____	1400 _____	2000 _____
0830 _____	1430 _____	2030 _____
0900 _____	1500 _____	2100 _____
0930 _____	1530 _____	2130 _____

SCHEDULE ENOUGH BREAKS? ☐   SCHEDULED M.I.N.S ☐

EVENING REVIEW

DID YOU ACCOMPLISH YOUR M.I.N.S. TODAY?   ☐ YES   ☐ NO

TODAY'S WINS

_____

_____

_____

TODAY I STRUGGLED WITH

_____

_____

_____

OPPORTUNITIES FOR IMPROVEMENT:
SCALE OF 1-10 HOW PRODUCTIVE WERE YOU TODAY?

PLANS FOR TOMORROW:

NOTES

DAILY PLAN

JAN FEB MAR APR MAY JUN JUL AUG SEP OCT NOV DEC
1 2 3 4 5 6 7 8 9 10 11 12 13 14 15 16 17 18 19 20 21 22 23 24 25 26 27 28 29 30 31

MORNING ROUTINE

THREE THINGS I AM GRATEFUL FOR:

_____

_____

_____

THREE THINGS I AM EXCITED FOR:

_____

_____

_____

WOKE UP: _____   HOURS SLEPT: _____   HIT SNOOZE? ▪Y ▪N

FOCUS	TODAY'S PT	REJUVENATE

GOAL #1
WEEKLY OBJECTIVE:
M.I.N.S.:

GOAL #2
WEEKLY OBJECTIVE:
M.I.N.S.:

GOAL #3
WEEKLY OBJECTIVE:
M.I.N.S.:

IF I DO THESE THREE THINGS TODAY I WILL WIN THE DAY!

1 _____

2 _____

3 _____

TIME BLOCKING

0400	1000	1600
0430	1030	1630
0500	1100	1700
0530	1130	1730
0600	1200	1800
0630	1230	1830
0700	1300	1900
0730	1330	1930
0800	1400	2000
0830	1430	2030
0900	1500	2100
0930	1530	2130

SCHEDULE ENOUGH BREAKS?   SCHEDULED M.I.N.S

EVENING REVIEW

DID YOU ACCOMPLISH YOUR M.I.N.S. TODAY?   YES   NO

TODAY'S WINS

TODAY I STRUGGLED WITH

OPPORTUNITIES FOR IMPROVEMENT:
SCALE OF 1-10 HOW PRODUCTIVE WERE YOU TODAY?

PLANS FOR TOMORROW:

NOTES

DAILY PLAN

JAN FEB MAR APR MAY JUN JUL AUG SEP OCT NOV DEC
1 2 3 4 5 6 7 8 9 10 11 12 13 14 15 16 17 18 19 20 21 22 23 24 25 26 27 28 29 30 31

MORNING ROUTINE

THREE THINGS I AM GRATEFUL FOR:

_____

_____

_____

THREE THINGS I AM EXCITED FOR:

_____

_____

_____

WOKE UP: _____   HOURS SLEPT: _____   HIT SNOOZE? ■ Y ■ N

FOCUS	TODAY'S PT	REJUVENATE

GOAL #1
WEEKLY OBJECTIVE:
M.I.N.S.:

GOAL #2
WEEKLY OBJECTIVE:
M.I.N.S.:

GOAL #3
WEEKLY OBJECTIVE:
M.I.N.S.:

IF I DO THESE THREE THINGS TODAY I WILL WIN THE DAY!

1 _____

2 _____

3 _____

TIME BLOCKING

0400	1000	1600
0430	1030	1630
0500	1100	1700
0530	1130	1730
0600	1200	1800
0630	1230	1830
0700	1300	1900
0730	1330	1930
0800	1400	2000
0830	1430	2030
0900	1500	2100
0930	1530	2130

SCHEDULE ENOUGH BREAKS? ▢   SCHEDULED M.I.N.S ▢

EVENING REVIEW

DID YOU ACCOMPLISH YOUR M.I.N.S. TODAY?   ▢ YES   ▢ NO

TODAY'S WINS

_____

_____

_____

TODAY I STRUGGLED WITH

_____

_____

_____

OPPORTUNITIES FOR IMPROVEMENT:
SCALE OF 1-10 HOW PRODUCTIVE WERE YOU TODAY?

PLANS FOR TOMORROW:

NOTES

DAILY PLAN

JAN FEB MAR APR MAY JUN JUL AUG SEP OCT NOV DEC
1 2 3 4 5 6 7 8 9 10 11 12 13 14 15 16 17 18 19 20 21 22 23 24 25 26 27 28 29 30 31

MORNING ROUTINE

THREE THINGS I AM GRATEFUL FOR:

_____

_____

_____

THREE THINGS I AM EXCITED FOR:

_____

_____

_____

WOKE UP: _____   HOURS SLEPT: _____   HIT SNOOZE? ■ Y ■ N

FOCUS	TODAY'S PT	REJUVENATE

GOAL #1 _____
WEEKLY OBJECTIVE:
M.I.N.S.:

GOAL #2 _____
WEEKLY OBJECTIVE:
M.I.N.S.:

GOAL #3 _____
WEEKLY OBJECTIVE:
M.I.N.S.:

IF I DO THESE THREE THINGS TODAY I WILL WIN THE DAY!

1. _____
2. _____
3. _____

TIME BLOCKING

0400 _____	1000 _____	1600 _____
0430 _____	1030 _____	1630 _____
0500 _____	1100 _____	1700 _____
0530 _____	1130 _____	1730 _____
0600 _____	1200 _____	1800 _____
0630 _____	1230 _____	1830 _____
0700 _____	1300 _____	1900 _____
0730 _____	1330 _____	1930 _____
0800 _____	1400 _____	2000 _____
0830 _____	1430 _____	2030 _____
0900 _____	1500 _____	2100 _____
0930 _____	1530 _____	2130 _____

SCHEDULE ENOUGH BREAKS? ☐   SCHEDULED M.I.N.S ☐

EVENING REVIEW

DID YOU ACCOMPLISH YOUR M.I.N.S. TODAY?   ☐ YES   ☐ NO

TODAY'S WINS

_____

_____

_____

TODAY I STRUGGLED WITH

_____

_____

_____

OPPORTUNITIES FOR IMPROVEMENT:
SCALE OF 1-10 HOW PRODUCTIVE WERE YOU TODAY?

PLANS FOR TOMORROW:

NOTES

DAILY PLAN

JAN FEB MAR APR MAY JUN JUL AUG SEP OCT NOV DEC
1 2 3 4 5 6 7 8 9 10 11 12 13 14 15 16 17 18 19 20 21 22 23 24 25 26 27 28 29 30 31

MORNING ROUTINE

THREE THINGS I AM GRATEFUL FOR:

_____

_____

_____

THREE THINGS I AM EXCITED FOR:

_____

_____

_____

WOKE UP: _____   HOURS SLEPT: _____   HIT SNOOZE? ■ Y ■ N

FOCUS	TODAY'S PT	REJUVENATE

GOAL #1
WEEKLY OBJECTIVE:
M.I.N.S.:

GOAL #2
WEEKLY OBJECTIVE:
M.I.N.S.:

GOAL #3
WEEKLY OBJECTIVE:
M.I.N.S.:

IF I DO THESE THREE THINGS TODAY I WILL WIN THE DAY!

1 _____

2 _____

3 _____

TIME BLOCKING

0400	1000	1600
0430	1030	1630
0500	1100	1700
0530	1130	1730
0600	1200	1800
0630	1230	1830
0700	1300	1900
0730	1330	1930
0800	1400	2000
0830	1430	2030
0900	1500	2100
0930	1530	2130

SCHEDULE ENOUGH BREAKS? ☐   SCHEDULED M.I.N.S ☐

EVENING REVIEW

DID YOU ACCOMPLISH YOUR M.I.N.S. TODAY?   ☐ YES   ☐ NO

TODAY'S WINS

_____

_____

_____

TODAY I STRUGGLED WITH

_____

_____

_____

OPPORTUNITIES FOR IMPROVEMENT:
SCALE OF 1-10 HOW PRODUCTIVE WERE YOU TODAY?

PLANS FOR TOMORROW:

NOTES

DAILY PLAN

JAN FEB MAR APR MAY JUN JUL AUG SEP OCT NOV DEC
1 2 3 4 5 6 7 8 9 10 11 12 13 14 15 16 17 18 19 20 21 22 23 24 25 26 27 28 29 30 31

MORNING ROUTINE

THREE THINGS I AM
GRATEFUL FOR:

_____

_____

_____

THREE THINGS I AM
EXCITED FOR:

_____

_____

_____

WOKE UP: _____   HOURS SLEPT: _____   HIT SNOOZE? ■ Y ■ N

FOCUS	TODAY'S PT	REJUVENATE

GOAL #1 _____
WEEKLY OBJECTIVE:
M.I.N.S.:

GOAL #2 _____
WEEKLY OBJECTIVE:
M.I.N.S.:

GOAL #3 _____
WEEKLY OBJECTIVE:
M.I.N.S.:

IF I DO THESE THREE THINGS TODAY I WILL WIN THE DAY!

1 _____

2 _____

3 _____

TIME BLOCKING

0400	1000	1600
0430	1030	1630
0500	1100	1700
0530	1130	1730
0600	1200	1800
0630	1230	1830
0700	1300	1900
0730	1330	1930
0800	1400	2000
0830	1430	2030
0900	1500	2100
0930	1530	2130

SCHEDULE ENOUGH BREAKS? ☐   SCHEDULED M.I.N.S ☐

EVENING REVIEW

DID YOU ACCOMPLISH YOUR M.I.N.S. TODAY?   ☐ YES   ☐ NO

TODAY'S WINS

_____

_____

_____

TODAY I STRUGGLED WITH

_____

_____

_____

OPPORTUNITIES FOR IMPROVEMENT:
SCALE OF 1-10 HOW PRODUCTIVE WERE YOU TODAY?

PLANS FOR TOMORROW:

NOTES

DAILY PLAN

JAN FEB MAR APR MAY JUN JUL AUG SEP OCT NOV DEC
1 2 3 4 5 6 7 8 9 10 11 12 13 14 15 16 17 18 19 20 21 22 23 24 25 26 27 28 29 30 31

MORNING ROUTINE

THREE THINGS I AM GRATEFUL FOR:

_____

_____

_____

THREE THINGS I AM EXCITED FOR:

_____

_____

_____

WOKE UP: _____   HOURS SLEPT: _____   HIT SNOOZE? ☐ Y ☐ N

FOCUS	TODAY'S PT	REJUVENATE

GOAL #1
WEEKLY OBJECTIVE:
M.I.N.S.:

GOAL #2
WEEKLY OBJECTIVE:
M.I.N.S.:

GOAL #3
WEEKLY OBJECTIVE:
M.I.N.S.:

IF I DO THESE THREE THINGS TODAY I WILL WIN THE DAY!

1 _____

2 _____

3 _____

TIME BLOCKING

0400 _____	1000 _____	1600 _____
0430 _____	1030 _____	1630 _____
0500 _____	1100 _____	1700 _____
0530 _____	1130 _____	1730 _____
0600 _____	1200 _____	1800 _____
0630 _____	1230 _____	1830 _____
0700 _____	1300 _____	1900 _____
0730 _____	1330 _____	1930 _____
0800 _____	1400 _____	2000 _____
0830 _____	1430 _____	2030 _____
0900 _____	1500 _____	2100 _____
0930 _____	1530 _____	2130 _____

SCHEDULE ENOUGH BREAKS? ☐   SCHEDULED M.I.N.S ☐

EVENING REVIEW

DID YOU ACCOMPLISH YOUR M.I.N.S. TODAY?   ☐ YES   ☐ NO

TODAY'S WINS

_____

_____

_____

TODAY I STRUGGLED WITH

_____

_____

_____

OPPORTUNITIES FOR IMPROVEMENT:
SCALE OF 1-10 HOW PRODUCTIVE WERE YOU TODAY?

PLANS FOR TOMORROW:

NOTES

DAILY PLAN

JAN FEB MAR APR MAY JUN JUL AUG SEP OCT NOV DEC
1 2 3 4 5 6 7 8 9 10 11 12 13 14 15 16 17 18 19 20 21 22 23 24 25 26 27 28 29 30 31

MORNING ROUTINE

THREE THINGS I AM GRATEFUL FOR:

_____

_____

_____

THREE THINGS I AM EXCITED FOR:

_____

_____

_____

WOKE UP: _____   HOURS SLEPT: _____   HIT SNOOZE? ■Y ■N

FOCUS	TODAY'S PT	REJUVENATE

GOAL #1 _____
WEEKLY OBJECTIVE:
M.I.N.S.:

GOAL #2 _____
WEEKLY OBJECTIVE:
M.I.N.S.:

GOAL #3 _____
WEEKLY OBJECTIVE:
M.I.N.S.:

IF I DO THESE THREE THINGS TODAY I WILL WIN THE DAY!

1 _____

2 _____

3 _____

TIME BLOCKING

0400	1000	1600
0430	1030	1630
0500	1100	1700
0530	1130	1730
0600	1200	1800
0630	1230	1830
0700	1300	1900
0730	1330	1930
0800	1400	2000
0830	1430	2030
0900	1500	2100
0930	1530	2130

SCHEDULE ENOUGH BREAKS? ☐   SCHEDULED M.I.N.S ☐

EVENING REVIEW

DID YOU ACCOMPLISH YOUR M.I.N.S. TODAY?   ☐ YES   ☐ NO

TODAY'S WINS

_____

_____

_____

TODAY I STRUGGLED WITH

_____

_____

_____

OPPORTUNITIES FOR IMPROVEMENT:
SCALE OF 1-10 HOW PRODUCTIVE WERE YOU TODAY?

PLANS FOR TOMORROW:

NOTES

DAILY PLAN

JAN FEB MAR APR MAY JUN JUL AUG SEP OCT NOV DEC
1 2 3 4 5 6 7 8 9 10 11 12 13 14 15 16 17 18 19 20 21 22 23 24 25 26 27 28 29 30 31

MORNING ROUTINE

THREE THINGS I AM GRATEFUL FOR:

_____

_____

_____

THREE THINGS I AM EXCITED FOR:

_____

_____

_____

WOKE UP: _____   HOURS SLEPT: _____   HIT SNOOZE? ☐ Y ☐ N

FOCUS	TODAY'S PT	REJUVENATE

GOAL #1 _____
WEEKLY OBJECTIVE:
M.I.N.S.:

GOAL #2 _____
WEEKLY OBJECTIVE:
M.I.N.S.:

GOAL #3 _____
WEEKLY OBJECTIVE:
M.I.N.S.:

IF I DO THESE THREE THINGS TODAY I WILL WIN THE DAY!

1 _____

2 _____

3 _____

TIME BLOCKING

0400	1000	1600
0430	1030	1630
0500	1100	1700
0530	1130	1730
0600	1200	1800
0630	1230	1830
0700	1300	1900
0730	1330	1930
0800	1400	2000
0830	1430	2030
0900	1500	2100
0930	1530	2130

SCHEDULE ENOUGH BREAKS? ☐   SCHEDULED M.I.N.S ☐

EVENING REVIEW

DID YOU ACCOMPLISH YOUR M.I.N.S. TODAY?   ☐ YES   ☐ NO

TODAY'S WINS

_____

_____

_____

TODAY I STRUGGLED WITH

_____

_____

_____

OPPORTUNITIES FOR IMPROVEMENT:
SCALE OF 1-10 HOW PRODUCTIVE WERE YOU TODAY?

PLANS FOR TOMORROW:

NOTES

DAILY PLAN

JAN FEB MAR APR MAY JUN JUL AUG SEP OCT NOV DEC
1 2 3 4 5 6 7 8 9 10 11 12 13 14 15 16 17 18 19 20 21 22 23 24 25 26 27 28 29 30 31

MORNING ROUTINE

THREE THINGS I AM GRATEFUL FOR:

_____

_____

_____

THREE THINGS I AM EXCITED FOR:

_____

_____

_____

WOKE UP: _____   HOURS SLEPT: _____   HIT SNOOZE? ■ Y ■ N

FOCUS	TODAY'S PT	REJUVENATE

GOAL #1
WEEKLY OBJECTIVE:
M.I.N.S.:

GOAL #2
WEEKLY OBJECTIVE:
M.I.N.S.:

GOAL #3
WEEKLY OBJECTIVE:
M.I.N.S.:

IF I DO THESE THREE THINGS TODAY I WILL WIN THE DAY!

1 _____

2 _____

3 _____

TIME BLOCKING

0400	1000	1600
0430	1030	1630
0500	1100	1700
0530	1130	1730
0600	1200	1800
0630	1230	1830
0700	1300	1900
0730	1330	1930
0800	1400	2000
0830	1430	2030
0900	1500	2100
0930	1530	2130

SCHEDULE ENOUGH BREAKS?   SCHEDULED M.I.N.S

EVENING REVIEW

DID YOU ACCOMPLISH YOUR M.I.N.S. TODAY?   YES   NO

TODAY'S WINS

_____

_____

_____

TODAY I STRUGGLED WITH

_____

_____

_____

OPPORTUNITIES FOR IMPROVEMENT:
SCALE OF 1-10 HOW PRODUCTIVE WERE YOU TODAY?

PLANS FOR TOMORROW:

NOTES

DAILY PLAN

JAN FEB MAR APR MAY JUN JUL AUG SEP OCT NOV DEC
1 2 3 4 5 6 7 8 9 10 11 12 13 14 15 16 17 18 19 20 21 22 23 24 25 26 27 28 29 30 31

MORNING ROUTINE

THREE THINGS I AM GRATEFUL FOR:

_____

_____

_____

THREE THINGS I AM EXCITED FOR:

_____

_____

_____

WOKE UP: _____   HOURS SLEPT: _____   HIT SNOOZE? ▪Y ▪N

FOCUS	TODAY'S PT	REJUVENATE

GOAL #1 _____
WEEKLY OBJECTIVE:
M.I.N.S.:

GOAL #2 _____
WEEKLY OBJECTIVE:
M.I.N.S.:

GOAL #3 _____
WEEKLY OBJECTIVE:
M.I.N.S.:

IF I DO THESE THREE THINGS TODAY I WILL WIN THE DAY!

1 _____

2 _____

3 _____

TIME BLOCKING

0400 _____	1000 _____	1600 _____
0430 _____	1030 _____	1630 _____
0500 _____	1100 _____	1700 _____
0530 _____	1130 _____	1730 _____
0600 _____	1200 _____	1800 _____
0630 _____	1230 _____	1830 _____
0700 _____	1300 _____	1900 _____
0730 _____	1330 _____	1930 _____
0800 _____	1400 _____	2000 _____
0830 _____	1430 _____	2030 _____
0900 _____	1500 _____	2100 _____
0930 _____	1530 _____	2130 _____

SCHEDULE ENOUGH BREAKS? ☐   SCHEDULED M.I.N.S ☐

EVENING REVIEW

DID YOU ACCOMPLISH YOUR M.I.N.S. TODAY?   ☐ YES   ☐ NO

TODAY'S WINS

_____

_____

_____

TODAY I STRUGGLED WITH

_____

_____

_____

OPPORTUNITIES FOR IMPROVEMENT:
SCALE OF 1-10 HOW PRODUCTIVE WERE YOU TODAY?

PLANS FOR TOMORROW:

NOTES

DAILY PLAN

JAN FEB MAR APR MAY JUN JUL AUG SEP OCT NOV DEC
1 2 3 4 5 6 7 8 9 10 11 12 13 14 15 16 17 18 19 20 21 22 23 24 25 26 27 28 29 30 31

MORNING ROUTINE

THREE THINGS I AM GRATEFUL FOR:

_____

_____

_____

THREE THINGS I AM EXCITED FOR:

_____

_____

_____

WOKE UP: _____   HOURS SLEPT: _____   HIT SNOOZE? ■Y ■N

FOCUS	TODAY'S PT	REJUVENATE

GOAL #1 _____

WEEKLY OBJECTIVE:
M.I.N.S.:

GOAL #2 _____

WEEKLY OBJECTIVE:
M.I.N.S.:

GOAL #3 _____

WEEKLY OBJECTIVE:
M.I.N.S.:

IF I DO THESE THREE THINGS TODAY I WILL WIN THE DAY!

1 _____

2 _____

3 _____

TIME BLOCKING

0400 _____	1000 _____	1600 _____
0430 _____	1030 _____	1630 _____
0500 _____	1100 _____	1700 _____
0530 _____	1130 _____	1730 _____
0600 _____	1200 _____	1800 _____
0630 _____	1230 _____	1830 _____
0700 _____	1300 _____	1900 _____
0730 _____	1330 _____	1930 _____
0800 _____	1400 _____	2000 _____
0830 _____	1430 _____	2030 _____
0900 _____	1500 _____	2100 _____
0930 _____	1530 _____	2130 _____

SCHEDULE ENOUGH BREAKS? ☐   SCHEDULED M.I.N.S ☐

EVENING REVIEW

DID YOU ACCOMPLISH YOUR M.I.N.S. TODAY?   ☐ YES   ☐ NO

TODAY'S WINS

_____

_____

_____

TODAY I STRUGGLED WITH

_____

_____

_____

OPPORTUNITIES FOR IMPROVEMENT:
SCALE OF 1-10 HOW PRODUCTIVE WERE YOU TODAY?

PLANS FOR TOMORROW:

NOTES

DAILY PLAN

JAN FEB MAR APR MAY JUN JUL AUG SEP OCT NOV DEC
1 2 3 4 5 6 7 8 9 10 11 12 13 14 15 16 17 18 19 20 21 22 23 24 25 26 27 28 29 30 31

MORNING ROUTINE

THREE THINGS I AM GRATEFUL FOR:

_____

_____

_____

THREE THINGS I AM EXCITED FOR:

_____

_____

_____

WOKE UP: _____   HOURS SLEPT: _____   HIT SNOOZE? ▪Y ▪N

FOCUS	TODAY'S PT	REJUVENATE

GOAL #1
WEEKLY OBJECTIVE:
M.I.N.S.:

GOAL #2
WEEKLY OBJECTIVE:
M.I.N.S.:

GOAL #3
WEEKLY OBJECTIVE:
M.I.N.S.:

IF I DO THESE THREE THINGS TODAY I WILL WIN THE DAY!

1 _____

2 _____

3 _____

TIME BLOCKING

0400	1000	1600
0430	1030	1630
0500	1100	1700
0530	1130	1730
0600	1200	1800
0630	1230	1830
0700	1300	1900
0730	1330	1930
0800	1400	2000
0830	1430	2030
0900	1500	2100
0930	1530	2130

SCHEDULE ENOUGH BREAKS? ☐   SCHEDULED M.I.N.S ☐

EVENING REVIEW

DID YOU ACCOMPLISH YOUR M.I.N.S. TODAY?   ☐ YES   ☐ NO

TODAY'S WINS

_____

_____

_____

TODAY I STRUGGLED WITH

_____

_____

_____

OPPORTUNITIES FOR IMPROVEMENT:
SCALE OF 1-10 HOW PRODUCTIVE WERE YOU TODAY?

PLANS FOR TOMORROW:

NOTES

DAILY PLAN

JAN FEB MAR APR MAY JUN JUL AUG SEP OCT NOV DEC
1 2 3 4 5 6 7 8 9 10 11 12 13 14 15 16 17 18 19 20 21 22 23 24 25 26 27 28 29 30 31

MORNING ROUTINE

THREE THINGS I AM GRATEFUL FOR:

_____

_____

_____

THREE THINGS I AM EXCITED FOR:

_____

_____

_____

WOKE UP: _____   HOURS SLEPT: _____   HIT SNOOZE? ■ Y ■ N

FOCUS	TODAY'S PT	REJUVENATE

GOAL #1 _____
WEEKLY OBJECTIVE:
M.I.N.S.:

GOAL #2 _____
WEEKLY OBJECTIVE:
M.I.N.S.:

GOAL #3 _____
WEEKLY OBJECTIVE:
M.I.N.S.:

IF I DO THESE THREE THINGS TODAY I WILL WIN THE DAY!

1. _____
2. _____
3. _____

TIME BLOCKING

0400	1000	1600
0430	1030	1630
0500	1100	1700
0530	1130	1730
0600	1200	1800
0630	1230	1830
0700	1300	1900
0730	1330	1930
0800	1400	2000
0830	1430	2030
0900	1500	2100
0930	1530	2130

SCHEDULE ENOUGH BREAKS? ☐   SCHEDULED M.I.N.S ☐

EVENING REVIEW

DID YOU ACCOMPLISH YOUR M.I.N.S. TODAY?   ☐ YES   ☐ NO

TODAY'S WINS

_____

_____

_____

TODAY I STRUGGLED WITH

_____

_____

_____

OPPORTUNITIES FOR IMPROVEMENT:
SCALE OF 1-10 HOW PRODUCTIVE WERE YOU TODAY?

PLANS FOR TOMORROW:

NOTES

DAILY PLAN

JAN FEB MAR APR MAY JUN JUL AUG SEP OCT NOV DEC
1 2 3 4 5 6 7 8 9 10 11 12 13 14 15 16 17 18 19 20 21 22 23 24 25 26 27 28 29 30 31

MORNING ROUTINE

THREE THINGS I AM GRATEFUL FOR:

_____

_____

_____

THREE THINGS I AM EXCITED FOR:

_____

_____

_____

WOKE UP: _____   HOURS SLEPT: _____   HIT SNOOZE? ☐ Y ☐ N

FOCUS	TODAY'S PT	REJUVENATE

GOAL #1 _____
WEEKLY OBJECTIVE:
M.I.N.S.:

GOAL #2 _____
WEEKLY OBJECTIVE:
M.I.N.S.:

GOAL #3 _____
WEEKLY OBJECTIVE:
M.I.N.S.:

IF I DO THESE THREE THINGS TODAY I WILL WIN THE DAY!

1 _____

2 _____

3 _____

TIME BLOCKING

0400 _____	1000 _____	1600 _____
0430 _____	1030 _____	1630 _____
0500 _____	1100 _____	1700 _____
0530 _____	1130 _____	1730 _____
0600 _____	1200 _____	1800 _____
0630 _____	1230 _____	1830 _____
0700 _____	1300 _____	1900 _____
0730 _____	1330 _____	1930 _____
0800 _____	1400 _____	2000 _____
0830 _____	1430 _____	2030 _____
0900 _____	1500 _____	2100 _____
0930 _____	1530 _____	2130 _____

SCHEDULE ENOUGH BREAKS? ☐   SCHEDULED M.I.N.S ☐

EVENING REVIEW

DID YOU ACCOMPLISH YOUR M.I.N.S. TODAY?   ☐ YES   ☐ NO

TODAY'S WINS

_____

_____

_____

TODAY I STRUGGLED WITH

_____

_____

_____

OPPORTUNITIES FOR IMPROVEMENT:
SCALE OF 1-10 HOW PRODUCTIVE WERE YOU TODAY?

PLANS FOR TOMORROW:

NOTES

DAILY PLAN

JAN FEB MAR APR MAY JUN JUL AUG SEP OCT NOV DEC
1 2 3 4 5 6 7 8 9 10 11 12 13 14 15 16 17 18 19 20 21 22 23 24 25 26 27 28 29 30 31

MORNING ROUTINE

THREE THINGS I AM GRATEFUL FOR:

_____

_____

_____

THREE THINGS I AM EXCITED FOR:

_____

_____

_____

WOKE UP: _____   HOURS SLEPT: _____   HIT SNOOZE? ■ Y ■ N

FOCUS	TODAY'S PT	REJUVENATE

GOAL #1
WEEKLY OBJECTIVE:
M.I.N.S.:

GOAL #2
WEEKLY OBJECTIVE:
M.I.N.S.:

GOAL #3
WEEKLY OBJECTIVE:
M.I.N.S.:

IF I DO THESE THREE THINGS TODAY I WILL WIN THE DAY!

1 _____

2 _____

3 _____

TIME BLOCKING

0400 _____	1000 _____	1600 _____
0430 _____	1030 _____	1630 _____
0500 _____	1100 _____	1700 _____
0530 _____	1130 _____	1730 _____
0600 _____	1200 _____	1800 _____
0630 _____	1230 _____	1830 _____
0700 _____	1300 _____	1900 _____
0730 _____	1330 _____	1930 _____
0800 _____	1400 _____	2000 _____
0830 _____	1430 _____	2030 _____
0900 _____	1500 _____	2100 _____
0930 _____	1530 _____	2130 _____

SCHEDULE ENOUGH BREAKS? ☐   SCHEDULED M.I.N.S ☐

EVENING REVIEW

DID YOU ACCOMPLISH YOUR M.I.N.S. TODAY?   ☐ YES   ☐ NO

TODAY'S WINS

_____

_____

_____

TODAY I STRUGGLED WITH

_____

_____

_____

OPPORTUNITIES FOR IMPROVEMENT:
SCALE OF 1-10 HOW PRODUCTIVE WERE YOU TODAY?

PLANS FOR TOMORROW:

NOTES

DAILY PLAN

JAN FEB MAR APR MAY JUN JUL AUG SEP OCT NOV DEC
1 2 3 4 5 6 7 8 9 10 11 12 13 14 15 16 17 18 19 20 21 22 23 24 25 26 27 28 29 30 31

MORNING ROUTINE

THREE THINGS I AM GRATEFUL FOR:

_____

_____

_____

THREE THINGS I AM EXCITED FOR:

_____

_____

_____

WOKE UP: _____   HOURS SLEPT: _____   HIT SNOOZE? ▪Y ▪N

FOCUS	TODAY'S PT	REJUVENATE

GOAL #1 _____
WEEKLY OBJECTIVE:
M.I.N.S.:

GOAL #2 _____
WEEKLY OBJECTIVE:
M.I.N.S.:

GOAL #3 _____
WEEKLY OBJECTIVE:
M.I.N.S.:

IF I DO THESE THREE THINGS TODAY I WILL WIN THE DAY!

1 _____

2 _____

3 _____

TIME BLOCKING

0400	1000	1600
0430	1030	1630
0500	1100	1700
0530	1130	1730
0600	1200	1800
0630	1230	1830
0700	1300	1900
0730	1330	1930
0800	1400	2000
0830	1430	2030
0900	1500	2100
0930	1530	2130

SCHEDULE ENOUGH BREAKS? ☐   SCHEDULED M.I.N.S ☐

EVENING REVIEW

DID YOU ACCOMPLISH YOUR M.I.N.S. TODAY?   ☐ YES   ☐ NO

TODAY'S WINS

_____

_____

_____

TODAY I STRUGGLED WITH

_____

_____

_____

OPPORTUNITIES FOR IMPROVEMENT:
SCALE OF 1-10 HOW PRODUCTIVE WERE YOU TODAY?

PLANS FOR TOMORROW:

NOTES

DAILY PLAN

JAN FEB MAR APR MAY JUN JUL AUG SEP OCT NOV DEC
1 2 3 4 5 6 7 8 9 10 11 12 13 14 15 16 17 18 19 20 21 22 23 24 25 26 27 28 29 30 31

MORNING ROUTINE

THREE THINGS I AM GRATEFUL FOR:

_____

_____

_____

THREE THINGS I AM EXCITED FOR:

_____

_____

_____

WOKE UP: _____   HOURS SLEPT: _____   HIT SNOOZE? ■Y ■N

FOCUS	TODAY'S PT	REJUVENATE

GOAL #1 _____
WEEKLY OBJECTIVE:
M.I.N.S.:

GOAL #2 _____
WEEKLY OBJECTIVE:
M.I.N.S.:

GOAL #3 _____
WEEKLY OBJECTIVE:
M.I.N.S.:

IF I DO THESE THREE THINGS TODAY I WILL WIN THE DAY!

1 _____

2 _____

3 _____

TIME BLOCKING

0400	1000	1600
0430	1030	1630
0500	1100	1700
0530	1130	1730
0600	1200	1800
0630	1230	1830
0700	1300	1900
0730	1330	1930
0800	1400	2000
0830	1430	2030
0900	1500	2100
0930	1530	2130

SCHEDULE ENOUGH BREAKS? ▢   SCHEDULED M.I.N.S ▢

EVENING REVIEW

DID YOU ACCOMPLISH YOUR M.I.N.S. TODAY?   ▢ YES   ▢ NO

TODAY'S WINS

___

___

___

TODAY I STRUGGLED WITH

___

___

___

OPPORTUNITIES FOR IMPROVEMENT:
SCALE OF 1-10 HOW PRODUCTIVE WERE YOU TODAY?

PLANS FOR TOMORROW:

NOTES

DAILY PLAN

JAN FEB MAR APR MAY JUN JUL AUG SEP OCT NOV DEC
1 2 3 4 5 6 7 8 9 10 11 12 13 14 15 16 17 18 19 20 21 22 23 24 25 26 27 28 29 30 31

MORNING ROUTINE

THREE THINGS I AM GRATEFUL FOR:

_____

_____

_____

THREE THINGS I AM EXCITED FOR:

_____

_____

_____

WOKE UP: _____ HOURS SLEPT: _____ HIT SNOOZE? ■ Y ■ N

FOCUS	TODAY'S PT	REJUVENATE

GOAL #1
WEEKLY OBJECTIVE:
M.I.N.S.:

GOAL #2
WEEKLY OBJECTIVE:
M.I.N.S.:

GOAL #3
WEEKLY OBJECTIVE:
M.I.N.S.:

IF I DO THESE THREE THINGS TODAY I WILL WIN THE DAY!

1 _____

2 _____

3 _____

TIME BLOCKING

0400 _____	1000 _____	1600 _____
0430 _____	1030 _____	1630 _____
0500 _____	1100 _____	1700 _____
0530 _____	1130 _____	1730 _____
0600 _____	1200 _____	1800 _____
0630 _____	1230 _____	1830 _____
0700 _____	1300 _____	1900 _____
0730 _____	1330 _____	1930 _____
0800 _____	1400 _____	2000 _____
0830 _____	1430 _____	2030 _____
0900 _____	1500 _____	2100 _____
0930 _____	1530 _____	2130 _____

SCHEDULE ENOUGH BREAKS? ☐   SCHEDULED M.I.N.S ☐

EVENING REVIEW

DID YOU ACCOMPLISH YOUR M.I.N.S. TODAY?   ☐ YES   ☐ NO

TODAY'S WINS

_____

_____

_____

TODAY I STRUGGLED WITH

_____

_____

_____

OPPORTUNITIES FOR IMPROVEMENT:
SCALE OF 1-10 HOW PRODUCTIVE WERE YOU TODAY?

PLANS FOR TOMORROW:

NOTES

DAILY PLAN

JAN FEB MAR APR MAY JUN JUL AUG SEP OCT NOV DEC
1 2 3 4 5 6 7 8 9 10 11 12 13 14 15 16 17 18 19 20 21 22 23 24 25 26 27 28 29 30 31

MORNING ROUTINE

THREE THINGS I AM GRATEFUL FOR:

_____

_____

_____

THREE THINGS I AM EXCITED FOR:

_____

_____

_____

WOKE UP: _____   HOURS SLEPT: _____   HIT SNOOZE? ▪Y ▪N

FOCUS	TODAY'S PT	REJUVENATE

GOAL #1
WEEKLY OBJECTIVE:
M.I.N.S.:

GOAL #2
WEEKLY OBJECTIVE:
M.I.N.S.:

GOAL #3
WEEKLY OBJECTIVE:
M.I.N.S.:

IF I DO THESE THREE THINGS TODAY I WILL WIN THE DAY!

1 _____

2 _____

3 _____

TIME BLOCKING

0400 _____	1000 _____	1600 _____
0430 _____	1030 _____	1630 _____
0500 _____	1100 _____	1700 _____
0530 _____	1130 _____	1730 _____
0600 _____	1200 _____	1800 _____
0630 _____	1230 _____	1830 _____
0700 _____	1300 _____	1900 _____
0730 _____	1330 _____	1930 _____
0800 _____	1400 _____	2000 _____
0830 _____	1430 _____	2030 _____
0900 _____	1500 _____	2100 _____
0930 _____	1530 _____	2130 _____

SCHEDULE ENOUGH BREAKS? ☐   SCHEDULED M.I.N.S ☐

EVENING REVIEW

DID YOU ACCOMPLISH YOUR M.I.N.S. TODAY?   ☐ YES   ☐ NO

TODAY'S WINS

_____

_____

_____

TODAY I STRUGGLED WITH

_____

_____

_____

OPPORTUNITIES FOR IMPROVEMENT: _____
SCALE OF 1-10 HOW PRODUCTIVE WERE YOU TODAY? _____

PLANS FOR TOMORROW:

NOTES

DAILY PLAN

JAN FEB MAR APR MAY JUN JUL AUG SEP OCT NOV DEC
1 2 3 4 5 6 7 8 9 10 11 12 13 14 15 16 17 18 19 20 21 22 23 24 25 26 27 28 29 30 31

MORNING ROUTINE

THREE THINGS I AM GRATEFUL FOR:

_____

_____

_____

THREE THINGS I AM EXCITED FOR:

_____

_____

_____

WOKE UP: _____   HOURS SLEPT: _____   HIT SNOOZE? ■ Y ■ N

FOCUS	TODAY'S PT	REJUVENATE

GOAL #1 _____
WEEKLY OBJECTIVE:
M.I.N.S.:

GOAL #2 _____
WEEKLY OBJECTIVE:
M.I.N.S.:

GOAL #3 _____
WEEKLY OBJECTIVE:
M.I.N.S.:

IF I DO THESE THREE THINGS TODAY I WILL WIN THE DAY!

1 _____

2 _____

3 _____

TIME BLOCKING

0400	1000	1600
0430	1030	1630
0500	1100	1700
0530	1130	1730
0600	1200	1800
0630	1230	1830
0700	1300	1900
0730	1330	1930
0800	1400	2000
0830	1430	2030
0900	1500	2100
0930	1530	2130

SCHEDULE ENOUGH BREAKS?　　　SCHEDULED M.I.N.S

EVENING REVIEW

DID YOU ACCOMPLISH YOUR M.I.N.S. TODAY?　　YES　　NO

TODAY'S WINS

TODAY I STRUGGLED WITH

_____　　_____

_____　　_____

_____　　_____

OPPORTUNITIES FOR IMPROVEMENT:
SCALE OF 1-10 HOW PRODUCTIVE WERE YOU TODAY?

PLANS FOR TOMORROW:

NOTES

DAILY PLAN

JAN FEB MAR APR MAY JUN JUL AUG SEP OCT NOV DEC
1 2 3 4 5 6 7 8 9 10 11 12 13 14 15 16 17 18 19 20 21 22 23 24 25 26 27 28 29 30 31

MORNING ROUTINE

THREE THINGS I AM GRATEFUL FOR:

_____

_____

_____

THREE THINGS I AM EXCITED FOR:

_____

_____

_____

WOKE UP: _____   HOURS SLEPT: _____   HIT SNOOZE? ▪Y ▪N

FOCUS	TODAY'S PT	REJUVENATE

GOAL #1 _____
WEEKLY OBJECTIVE:
M.I.N.S.:

GOAL #2 _____
WEEKLY OBJECTIVE:
M.I.N.S.:

GOAL #3 _____
WEEKLY OBJECTIVE:
M.I.N.S.:

IF I DO THESE THREE THINGS TODAY I WILL WIN THE DAY!

1. _____
2. _____
3. _____

TIME BLOCKING

0400 _____	1000 _____	1600 _____
0430 _____	1030 _____	1630 _____
0500 _____	1100 _____	1700 _____
0530 _____	1130 _____	1730 _____
0600 _____	1200 _____	1800 _____
0630 _____	1230 _____	1830 _____
0700 _____	1300 _____	1900 _____
0730 _____	1330 _____	1930 _____
0800 _____	1400 _____	2000 _____
0830 _____	1430 _____	2030 _____
0900 _____	1500 _____	2100 _____
0930 _____	1530 _____	2130 _____

SCHEDULE ENOUGH BREAKS? ☐   SCHEDULED M.I.N.S ☐

EVENING REVIEW

DID YOU ACCOMPLISH YOUR M.I.N.S. TODAY?   ☐ YES   ☐ NO

TODAY'S WINS

_____

_____

_____

TODAY I STRUGGLED WITH

_____

_____

_____

OPPORTUNITIES FOR IMPROVEMENT:
SCALE OF 1-10 HOW PRODUCTIVE WERE YOU TODAY?

PLANS FOR TOMORROW:

NOTES

DAILY PLAN

JAN FEB MAR APR MAY JUN JUL AUG SEP OCT NOV DEC
1 2 3 4 5 6 7 8 9 10 11 12 13 14 15 16 17 18 19 20 21 22 23 24 25 26 27 28 29 30 31

MORNING ROUTINE

THREE THINGS I AM GRATEFUL FOR:

_____

_____

_____

THREE THINGS I AM EXCITED FOR:

_____

_____

_____

WOKE UP: _____   HOURS SLEPT: _____   HIT SNOOZE? ■ Y ■ N

FOCUS	TODAY'S PT	REJUVENATE

GOAL #1 _____
WEEKLY OBJECTIVE:
M.I.N.S.:

GOAL #2 _____
WEEKLY OBJECTIVE:
M.I.N.S.:

GOAL #3 _____
WEEKLY OBJECTIVE:
M.I.N.S.:

IF I DO THESE THREE THINGS TODAY I WILL WIN THE DAY!

1 _____

2 _____

3 _____

TIME BLOCKING

0400	1000	1600
0430	1030	1630
0500	1100	1700
0530	1130	1730
0600	1200	1800
0630	1230	1830
0700	1300	1900
0730	1330	1930
0800	1400	2000
0830	1430	2030
0900	1500	2100
0930	1530	2130

SCHEDULE ENOUGH BREAKS? ▢   SCHEDULED M.I.N.S ▢

EVENING REVIEW

DID YOU ACCOMPLISH YOUR M.I.N.S. TODAY?   ▢ YES   ▢ NO

TODAY'S WINS

_____

_____

_____

TODAY I STRUGGLED WITH

_____

_____

_____

OPPORTUNITIES FOR IMPROVEMENT:
SCALE OF 1-10 HOW PRODUCTIVE WERE YOU TODAY?

PLANS FOR TOMORROW:

NOTES

DAILY PLAN

JAN FEB MAR APR MAY JUN JUL AUG SEP OCT NOV DEC
1 2 3 4 5 6 7 8 9 10 11 12 13 14 15 16 17 18 19 20 21 22 23 24 25 26 27 28 29 30 31

MORNING ROUTINE

THREE THINGS I AM
GRATEFUL FOR:

_____

_____

_____

THREE THINGS I AM
EXCITED FOR:

_____

_____

_____

WOKE UP: _____   HOURS SLEPT: _____   HIT SNOOZE? ☐ Y ☐ N

FOCUS	TODAY'S PT	REJUVENATE

GOAL #1 _____
WEEKLY OBJECTIVE:
M.I.N.S.:

GOAL #2 _____
WEEKLY OBJECTIVE:
M.I.N.S.:

GOAL #3 _____
WEEKLY OBJECTIVE:
M.I.N.S.:

IF I DO THESE THREE THINGS TODAY I WILL WIN THE DAY!

1 _____

2 _____

3 _____

TIME BLOCKING

0400 _____	1000 _____	1600 _____
0430 _____	1030 _____	1630 _____
0500 _____	1100 _____	1700 _____
0530 _____	1130 _____	1730 _____
0600 _____	1200 _____	1800 _____
0630 _____	1230 _____	1830 _____
0700 _____	1300 _____	1900 _____
0730 _____	1330 _____	1930 _____
0800 _____	1400 _____	2000 _____
0830 _____	1430 _____	2030 _____
0900 _____	1500 _____	2100 _____
0930 _____	1530 _____	2130 _____

SCHEDULE ENOUGH BREAKS? ☐   SCHEDULED M.I.N.S ☐

EVENING REVIEW

DID YOU ACCOMPLISH YOUR M.I.N.S. TODAY?   ☐ YES   ☐ NO

TODAY'S WINS

_____

_____

_____

TODAY I STRUGGLED WITH

_____

_____

_____

OPPORTUNITIES FOR IMPROVEMENT: _____

SCALE OF 1-10 HOW PRODUCTIVE WERE YOU TODAY? _____

PLANS FOR TOMORROW:

NOTES

DAILY PLAN

JAN FEB MAR APR MAY JUN JUL AUG SEP OCT NOV DEC
1 2 3 4 5 6 7 8 9 10 11 12 13 14 15 16 17 18 19 20 21 22 23 24 25 26 27 28 29 30 31

MORNING ROUTINE

THREE THINGS I AM GRATEFUL FOR:

_____

_____

_____

THREE THINGS I AM EXCITED FOR:

_____

_____

_____

WOKE UP: _____ HOURS SLEPT: _____ HIT SNOOZE? ■Y ■N

FOCUS	TODAY'S PT	REJUVENATE

GOAL #1
WEEKLY OBJECTIVE:
M.I.N.S.:

GOAL #2
WEEKLY OBJECTIVE:
M.I.N.S.:

GOAL #3
WEEKLY OBJECTIVE:
M.I.N.S.:

IF I DO THESE THREE THINGS TODAY I WILL WIN THE DAY!

1 _____

2 _____

3 _____

TIME BLOCKING

0400 _____	1000 _____	1600 _____
0430 _____	1030 _____	1630 _____
0500 _____	1100 _____	1700 _____
0530 _____	1130 _____	1730 _____
0600 _____	1200 _____	1800 _____
0630 _____	1230 _____	1830 _____
0700 _____	1300 _____	1900 _____
0730 _____	1330 _____	1930 _____
0800 _____	1400 _____	2000 _____
0830 _____	1430 _____	2030 _____
0900 _____	1500 _____	2100 _____
0930 _____	1530 _____	2130 _____

SCHEDULE ENOUGH BREAKS? ☐   SCHEDULED M.I.N.S ☐

EVENING REVIEW

DID YOU ACCOMPLISH YOUR M.I.N.S. TODAY?   ☐ YES   ☐ NO

TODAY'S WINS

_____

_____

_____

TODAY I STRUGGLED WITH

_____

_____

_____

OPPORTUNITIES FOR IMPROVEMENT:
SCALE OF 1-10 HOW PRODUCTIVE WERE YOU TODAY?

PLANS FOR TOMORROW:

NOTES

DAILY PLAN

JAN FEB MAR APR MAY JUN JUL AUG SEP OCT NOV DEC
1 2 3 4 5 6 7 8 9 10 11 12 13 14 15 16 17 18 19 20 21 22 23 24 25 26 27 28 29 30 31

MORNING ROUTINE

THREE THINGS I AM GRATEFUL FOR:

_____

_____

_____

THREE THINGS I AM EXCITED FOR:

_____

_____

_____

WOKE UP: _____   HOURS SLEPT: _____   HIT SNOOZE? ▪Y ▪N

FOCUS	TODAY'S PT	REJUVENATE

GOAL #1
WEEKLY OBJECTIVE:
M.I.N.S.:

GOAL #2
WEEKLY OBJECTIVE:
M.I.N.S.:

GOAL #3
WEEKLY OBJECTIVE:
M.I.N.S.:

IF I DO THESE THREE THINGS TODAY I WILL WIN THE DAY!

1. _____
2. _____
3. _____

TIME BLOCKING

0400	1000	1600
0430	1030	1630
0500	1100	1700
0530	1130	1730
0600	1200	1800
0630	1230	1830
0700	1300	1900
0730	1330	1930
0800	1400	2000
0830	1430	2030
0900	1500	2100
0930	1530	2130

SCHEDULE ENOUGH BREAKS? ☐   SCHEDULED M.I.N.S ☐

EVENING REVIEW

DID YOU ACCOMPLISH YOUR M.I.N.S. TODAY?   ☐ YES   ☐ NO

TODAY'S WINS

_____

_____

_____

TODAY I STRUGGLED WITH

_____

_____

_____

OPPORTUNITIES FOR IMPROVEMENT:
SCALE OF 1-10 HOW PRODUCTIVE WERE YOU TODAY?

PLANS FOR TOMORROW:

NOTES

DAILY PLAN

JAN FEB MAR APR MAY JUN JUL AUG SEP OCT NOV DEC
1 2 3 4 5 6 7 8 9 10 11 12 13 14 15 16 17 18 19 20 21 22 23 24 25 26 27 28 29 30 31

MORNING ROUTINE

THREE THINGS I AM GRATEFUL FOR:

_____

_____

_____

THREE THINGS I AM EXCITED FOR:

_____

_____

_____

WOKE UP: _____   HOURS SLEPT: _____   HIT SNOOZE? ■Y ■N

FOCUS	TODAY'S PT	REJUVENATE

GOAL #1
WEEKLY OBJECTIVE:
M.I.N.S.:

GOAL #2
WEEKLY OBJECTIVE:
M.I.N.S.:

GOAL #3
WEEKLY OBJECTIVE:
M.I.N.S.:

IF I DO THESE THREE THINGS TODAY I WILL WIN THE DAY!

1 _____

2 _____

3 _____

TIME BLOCKING

0400	1000	1600
0430	1030	1630
0500	1100	1700
0530	1130	1730
0600	1200	1800
0630	1230	1830
0700	1300	1900
0730	1330	1930
0800	1400	2000
0830	1430	2030
0900	1500	2100
0930	1530	2130

SCHEDULE ENOUGH BREAKS? ☐   SCHEDULED M.I.N.S ☐

EVENING REVIEW

DID YOU ACCOMPLISH YOUR M.I.N.S. TODAY?   ☐ YES   ☐ NO

TODAY'S WINS

_____

_____

_____

TODAY I STRUGGLED WITH

_____

_____

_____

OPPORTUNITIES FOR IMPROVEMENT:
SCALE OF 1-10 HOW PRODUCTIVE WERE YOU TODAY?

PLANS FOR TOMORROW:

NOTES

DAILY PLAN

JAN FEB MAR APR MAY JUN JUL AUG SEP OCT NOV DEC
1 2 3 4 5 6 7 8 9 10 11 12 13 14 15 16 17 18 19 20 21 22 23 24 25 26 27 28 29 30 31

MORNING ROUTINE

THREE THINGS I AM GRATEFUL FOR:

_____

_____

_____

THREE THINGS I AM EXCITED FOR:

_____

_____

_____

WOKE UP: _____   HOURS SLEPT: _____   HIT SNOOZE? ■ Y ■ N

FOCUS	TODAY'S PT	REJUVENATE

GOAL #1
WEEKLY OBJECTIVE:
M.I.N.S.:

GOAL #2
WEEKLY OBJECTIVE:
M.I.N.S.:

GOAL #3
WEEKLY OBJECTIVE:
M.I.N.S.:

IF I DO THESE THREE THINGS TODAY I WILL WIN THE DAY!

1 _____

2 _____

3 _____

TIME BLOCKING

0400 _____	1000 _____	1600 _____
0430 _____	1030 _____	1630 _____
0500 _____	1100 _____	1700 _____
0530 _____	1130 _____	1730 _____
0600 _____	1200 _____	1800 _____
0630 _____	1230 _____	1830 _____
0700 _____	1300 _____	1900 _____
0730 _____	1330 _____	1930 _____
0800 _____	1400 _____	2000 _____
0830 _____	1430 _____	2030 _____
0900 _____	1500 _____	2100 _____
0930 _____	1530 _____	2130 _____

SCHEDULE ENOUGH BREAKS? ☐   SCHEDULED M.I.N.S ☐

EVENING REVIEW

DID YOU ACCOMPLISH YOUR M.I.N.S. TODAY?   ☐ YES   ☐ NO

TODAY'S WINS

_____

_____

_____

TODAY I STRUGGLED WITH

_____

_____

_____

OPPORTUNITIES FOR IMPROVEMENT:
SCALE OF 1-10 HOW PRODUCTIVE WERE YOU TODAY?

PLANS FOR TOMORROW:

NOTES

DAILY PLAN

JAN FEB MAR APR MAY JUN JUL AUG SEP OCT NOV DEC
1 2 3 4 5 6 7 8 9 10 11 12 13 14 15 16 17 18 19 20 21 22 23 24 25 26 27 28 29 30 31

MORNING ROUTINE

THREE THINGS I AM GRATEFUL FOR:

_____

_____

_____

THREE THINGS I AM EXCITED FOR:

_____

_____

_____

WOKE UP: _____ HOURS SLEPT: _____ HIT SNOOZE? ■Y ■N

FOCUS	TODAY'S PT	REJUVENATE

GOAL #1
WEEKLY OBJECTIVE:
M.I.N.S.:

GOAL #2
WEEKLY OBJECTIVE:
M.I.N.S.:

GOAL #3
WEEKLY OBJECTIVE:
M.I.N.S.:

IF I DO THESE THREE THINGS TODAY I WILL WIN THE DAY!

1. _____
2. _____
3. _____

TIME BLOCKING

0400 _____	1000 _____	1600 _____
0430 _____	1030 _____	1630 _____
0500 _____	1100 _____	1700 _____
0530 _____	1130 _____	1730 _____
0600 _____	1200 _____	1800 _____
0630 _____	1230 _____	1830 _____
0700 _____	1300 _____	1900 _____
0730 _____	1330 _____	1930 _____
0800 _____	1400 _____	2000 _____
0830 _____	1430 _____	2030 _____
0900 _____	1500 _____	2100 _____
0930 _____	1530 _____	2130 _____

SCHEDULE ENOUGH BREAKS? ☐   SCHEDULED M.I.N.S ☐

EVENING REVIEW

DID YOU ACCOMPLISH YOUR M.I.N.S. TODAY?   ☐ YES   ☐ NO

TODAY'S WINS

_____

_____

_____

TODAY I STRUGGLED WITH

_____

_____

_____

OPPORTUNITIES FOR IMPROVEMENT:
SCALE OF 1-10 HOW PRODUCTIVE WERE YOU TODAY?

PLANS FOR TOMORROW:

NOTES

DAILY PLAN

JAN FEB MAR APR MAY JUN JUL AUG SEP OCT NOV DEC
1 2 3 4 5 6 7 8 9 10 11 12 13 14 15 16 17 18 19 20 21 22 23 24 25 26 27 28 29 30 31

MORNING ROUTINE

THREE THINGS I AM
GRATEFUL FOR:

_____

_____

_____

THREE THINGS I AM
EXCITED FOR:

_____

_____

_____

WOKE UP: _____ HOURS SLEPT: _____ HIT SNOOZE? ■ Y ■ N

FOCUS	TODAY'S PT	REJUVENATE

GOAL #1 _____
WEEKLY OBJECTIVE:
M.I.N.S.:

GOAL #2 _____
WEEKLY OBJECTIVE:
M.I.N.S.:

GOAL #3 _____
WEEKLY OBJECTIVE:
M.I.N.S.:

IF I DO THESE THREE THINGS TODAY I WILL WIN THE DAY!

1 _____

2 _____

3 _____

TIME BLOCKING

0400	1000	1600
0430	1030	1630
0500	1100	1700
0530	1130	1730
0600	1200	1800
0630	1230	1830
0700	1300	1900
0730	1330	1930
0800	1400	2000
0830	1430	2030
0900	1500	2100
0930	1530	2130

SCHEDULE ENOUGH BREAKS?   SCHEDULED M.I.N.S

EVENING REVIEW

DID YOU ACCOMPLISH YOUR M.I.N.S. TODAY?   YES   NO

TODAY'S WINS

_____

_____

_____

TODAY I STRUGGLED WITH

_____

_____

_____

OPPORTUNITIES FOR IMPROVEMENT:
SCALE OF 1-10 HOW PRODUCTIVE WERE YOU TODAY?

PLANS FOR TOMORROW:

NOTES

DAILY PLAN

JAN FEB MAR APR MAY JUN JUL AUG SEP OCT NOV DEC
1 2 3 4 5 6 7 8 9 10 11 12 13 14 15 16 17 18 19 20 21 22 23 24 25 26 27 28 29 30 31

MORNING ROUTINE

THREE THINGS I AM GRATEFUL FOR:

_____

_____

_____

THREE THINGS I AM EXCITED FOR:

_____

_____

_____

WOKE UP: _____ HOURS SLEPT: _____ HIT SNOOZE? ■ Y ■ N

FOCUS	TODAY'S PT	REJUVENATE

GOAL #1
WEEKLY OBJECTIVE:
M.I.N.S.:

GOAL #2
WEEKLY OBJECTIVE:
M.I.N.S.:

GOAL #3
WEEKLY OBJECTIVE:
M.I.N.S.:

IF I DO THESE THREE THINGS TODAY I WILL WIN THE DAY!

1 _____

2 _____

3 _____

TIME BLOCKING

0400	1000	1600
0430	1030	1630
0500	1100	1700
0530	1130	1730
0600	1200	1800
0630	1230	1830
0700	1300	1900
0730	1330	1930
0800	1400	2000
0830	1430	2030
0900	1500	2100
0930	1530	2130

SCHEDULE ENOUGH BREAKS? ☐   SCHEDULED M.I.N.S ☐

EVENING REVIEW

DID YOU ACCOMPLISH YOUR M.I.N.S. TODAY?   ☐ YES   ☐ NO

TODAY'S WINS

_____

_____

_____

TODAY I STRUGGLED WITH

_____

_____

_____

OPPORTUNITIES FOR IMPROVEMENT:
SCALE OF 1-10 HOW PRODUCTIVE WERE YOU TODAY?

PLANS FOR TOMORROW:

NOTES

DAILY PLAN

JAN FEB MAR APR MAY JUN JUL AUG SEP OCT NOV DEC
1 2 3 4 5 6 7 8 9 10 11 12 13 14 15 16 17 18 19 20 21 22 23 24 25 26 27 28 29 30 31

MORNING ROUTINE

THREE THINGS I AM
GRATEFUL FOR:

_____

_____

_____

THREE THINGS I AM
EXCITED FOR:

_____

_____

_____

WOKE UP: _____   HOURS SLEPT: _____   HIT SNOOZE? ■ Y ■ N

FOCUS	TODAY'S PT	REJUVENATE

GOAL #1
WEEKLY OBJECTIVE:
M.I.N.S.:

GOAL #2
WEEKLY OBJECTIVE:
M.I.N.S.:

GOAL #3
WEEKLY OBJECTIVE:
M.I.N.S.:

IF I DO THESE THREE THINGS TODAY I WILL WIN THE DAY!

1 _____

2 _____

3 _____

TIME BLOCKING

0400 _____	1000 _____	1600 _____
0430 _____	1030 _____	1630 _____
0500 _____	1100 _____	1700 _____
0530 _____	1130 _____	1730 _____
0600 _____	1200 _____	1800 _____
0630 _____	1230 _____	1830 _____
0700 _____	1300 _____	1900 _____
0730 _____	1330 _____	1930 _____
0800 _____	1400 _____	2000 _____
0830 _____	1430 _____	2030 _____
0900 _____	1500 _____	2100 _____
0930 _____	1530 _____	2130 _____

SCHEDULE ENOUGH BREAKS? ☐   SCHEDULED M.I.N.S ☐

EVENING REVIEW

DID YOU ACCOMPLISH YOUR M.I.N.S. TODAY?   ☐ YES   ☐ NO

TODAY'S WINS

_____

_____

_____

TODAY I STRUGGLED WITH

_____

_____

_____

OPPORTUNITIES FOR IMPROVEMENT:
SCALE OF 1-10 HOW PRODUCTIVE WERE YOU TODAY?

PLANS FOR TOMORROW:

NOTES

DAILY PLAN

JAN FEB MAR APR MAY JUN JUL AUG SEP OCT NOV DEC
1 2 3 4 5 6 7 8 9 10 11 12 13 14 15 16 17 18 19 20 21 22 23 24 25 26 27 28 29 30 31

MORNING ROUTINE

THREE THINGS I AM GRATEFUL FOR:

_____

_____

_____

THREE THINGS I AM EXCITED FOR:

_____

_____

_____

WOKE UP: ☐   HOURS SLEPT: ☐   HIT SNOOZE? ☐ Y ☐ N

FOCUS	TODAY'S PT	REJUVENATE

GOAL #1 _____
WEEKLY OBJECTIVE:
M.I.N.S.:

GOAL #2 _____
WEEKLY OBJECTIVE:
M.I.N.S.:

GOAL #3 _____
WEEKLY OBJECTIVE:
M.I.N.S.:

IF I DO THESE THREE THINGS TODAY I WILL WIN THE DAY!

1 _____

2 _____

3 _____

TIME BLOCKING

0400 _____	1000 _____	1600 _____
0430 _____	1030 _____	1630 _____
0500 _____	1100 _____	1700 _____
0530 _____	1130 _____	1730 _____
0600 _____	1200 _____	1800 _____
0630 _____	1230 _____	1830 _____
0700 _____	1300 _____	1900 _____
0730 _____	1330 _____	1930 _____
0800 _____	1400 _____	2000 _____
0830 _____	1430 _____	2030 _____
0900 _____	1500 _____	2100 _____
0930 _____	1530 _____	2130 _____

SCHEDULE ENOUGH BREAKS? ☐   SCHEDULED M.I.N.S ☐

EVENING REVIEW

DID YOU ACCOMPLISH YOUR M.I.N.S. TODAY?   ☐ YES   ☐ NO

TODAY'S WINS

_____

_____

_____

TODAY I STRUGGLED WITH

_____

_____

_____

OPPORTUNITIES FOR IMPROVEMENT:
SCALE OF 1-10 HOW PRODUCTIVE WERE YOU TODAY?

PLANS FOR TOMORROW:

NOTES

DAILY PLAN

JAN FEB MAR APR MAY JUN JUL AUG SEP OCT NOV DEC
1 2 3 4 5 6 7 8 9 10 11 12 13 14 15 16 17 18 19 20 21 22 23 24 25 26 27 28 29 30 31

MORNING ROUTINE

THREE THINGS I AM GRATEFUL FOR:

_____

_____

_____

THREE THINGS I AM EXCITED FOR:

_____

_____

_____

WOKE UP: _____   HOURS SLEPT: _____   HIT SNOOZE? ■ Y ■ N

FOCUS	TODAY'S PT	REJUVENATE

GOAL #1
WEEKLY OBJECTIVE:
M.I.N.S.:

GOAL #2
WEEKLY OBJECTIVE:
M.I.N.S.:

GOAL #3
WEEKLY OBJECTIVE:
M.I.N.S.:

IF I DO THESE THREE THINGS TODAY I WILL WIN THE DAY!

1 _____

2 _____

3 _____

TIME BLOCKING

0400 _____	1000 _____	1600 _____
0430 _____	1030 _____	1630 _____
0500 _____	1100 _____	1700 _____
0530 _____	1130 _____	1730 _____
0600 _____	1200 _____	1800 _____
0630 _____	1230 _____	1830 _____
0700 _____	1300 _____	1900 _____
0730 _____	1330 _____	1930 _____
0800 _____	1400 _____	2000 _____
0830 _____	1430 _____	2030 _____
0900 _____	1500 _____	2100 _____
0930 _____	1530 _____	2130 _____

SCHEDULE ENOUGH BREAKS? ☐   SCHEDULED M.I.N.S ☐

EVENING REVIEW

DID YOU ACCOMPLISH YOUR M.I.N.S. TODAY?   ☐ YES   ☐ NO

TODAY'S WINS

_____

_____

_____

TODAY I STRUGGLED WITH

_____

_____

_____

OPPORTUNITIES FOR IMPROVEMENT: _____
SCALE OF 1-10 HOW PRODUCTIVE WERE YOU TODAY? _____

PLANS FOR TOMORROW:

NOTES

DAILY PLAN

JAN FEB MAR APR MAY JUN JUL AUG SEP OCT NOV DEC
1 2 3 4 5 6 7 8 9 10 11 12 13 14 15 16 17 18 19 20 21 22 23 24 25 26 27 28 29 30 31

MORNING ROUTINE

THREE THINGS I AM GRATEFUL FOR:

_____

_____

_____

THREE THINGS I AM EXCITED FOR:

_____

_____

_____

WOKE UP: _____ HOURS SLEPT: _____ HIT SNOOZE? ▪Y ▪N

FOCUS	TODAY'S PT	REJUVENATE

GOAL #1
WEEKLY OBJECTIVE:
M.I.N.S.:

GOAL #2
WEEKLY OBJECTIVE:
M.I.N.S.:

GOAL #3
WEEKLY OBJECTIVE:
M.I.N.S.:

IF I DO THESE THREE THINGS TODAY I WILL WIN THE DAY!

1. _____
2. _____
3. _____

TIME BLOCKING

0400 _____	1000 _____	1600 _____
0430 _____	1030 _____	1630 _____
0500 _____	1100 _____	1700 _____
0530 _____	1130 _____	1730 _____
0600 _____	1200 _____	1800 _____
0630 _____	1230 _____	1830 _____
0700 _____	1300 _____	1900 _____
0730 _____	1330 _____	1930 _____
0800 _____	1400 _____	2000 _____
0830 _____	1430 _____	2030 _____
0900 _____	1500 _____	2100 _____
0930 _____	1530 _____	2130 _____

SCHEDULE ENOUGH BREAKS? ☐   SCHEDULED M.I.N.S ☐

EVENING REVIEW

DID YOU ACCOMPLISH YOUR M.I.N.S. TODAY?   ☐ YES   ☐ NO

TODAY'S WINS

_____

_____

_____

TODAY I STRUGGLED WITH

_____

_____

_____

OPPORTUNITIES FOR IMPROVEMENT:
SCALE OF 1-10 HOW PRODUCTIVE WERE YOU TODAY?

PLANS FOR TOMORROW:

NOTES

DAILY PLAN

JAN FEB MAR APR MAY JUN JUL AUG SEP OCT NOV DEC
1 2 3 4 5 6 7 8 9 10 11 12 13 14 15 16 17 18 19 20 21 22 23 24 25 26 27 28 29 30 31

MORNING ROUTINE

THREE THINGS I AM GRATEFUL FOR:

_____

_____

_____

THREE THINGS I AM EXCITED FOR:

_____

_____

_____

WOKE UP: _____   HOURS SLEPT: _____   HIT SNOOZE? ■Y ■N

FOCUS	TODAY'S PT	REJUVENATE

GOAL #1 _____
WEEKLY OBJECTIVE:
M.I.N.S.:

GOAL #2 _____
WEEKLY OBJECTIVE:
M.I.N.S.:

GOAL #3 _____
WEEKLY OBJECTIVE:
M.I.N.S.:

IF I DO THESE THREE THINGS TODAY I WILL WIN THE DAY!

1 _____

2 _____

3 _____

TIME BLOCKING

0400	1000	1600
0430	1030	1630
0500	1100	1700
0530	1130	1730
0600	1200	1800
0630	1230	1830
0700	1300	1900
0730	1330	1930
0800	1400	2000
0830	1430	2030
0900	1500	2100
0930	1530	2130

SCHEDULE ENOUGH BREAKS? ☐   SCHEDULED M.I.N.S ☐

EVENING REVIEW

DID YOU ACCOMPLISH YOUR M.I.N.S. TODAY?   ☐ YES   ☐ NO

TODAY'S WINS

_____

_____

_____

TODAY I STRUGGLED WITH

_____

_____

_____

OPPORTUNITIES FOR IMPROVEMENT:
SCALE OF 1-10 HOW PRODUCTIVE WERE YOU TODAY?

PLANS FOR TOMORROW:

NOTES

DAILY PLAN

JAN FEB MAR APR MAY JUN JUL AUG SEP OCT NOV DEC
1 2 3 4 5 6 7 8 9 10 11 12 13 14 15 16 17 18 19 20 21 22 23 24 25 26 27 28 29 30 31

MORNING ROUTINE

THREE THINGS I AM GRATEFUL FOR:

_____

_____

_____

THREE THINGS I AM EXCITED FOR:

_____

_____

_____

WOKE UP: _____   HOURS SLEPT: _____   HIT SNOOZE? ▪ Y ▪ N

FOCUS	TODAY'S PT	REJUVENATE

GOAL #1
WEEKLY OBJECTIVE:
M.I.N.S.:

GOAL #2
WEEKLY OBJECTIVE:
M.I.N.S.:

GOAL #3
WEEKLY OBJECTIVE:
M.I.N.S.:

IF I DO THESE THREE THINGS TODAY I WILL WIN THE DAY!

1. _____
2. _____
3. _____

TIME BLOCKING

0400 _____	1000 _____	1600 _____
0430 _____	1030 _____	1630 _____
0500 _____	1100 _____	1700 _____
0530 _____	1130 _____	1730 _____
0600 _____	1200 _____	1800 _____
0630 _____	1230 _____	1830 _____
0700 _____	1300 _____	1900 _____
0730 _____	1330 _____	1930 _____
0800 _____	1400 _____	2000 _____
0830 _____	1430 _____	2030 _____
0900 _____	1500 _____	2100 _____
0930 _____	1530 _____	2130 _____

SCHEDULE ENOUGH BREAKS? ☐   SCHEDULED M.I.N.S ☐

EVENING REVIEW

DID YOU ACCOMPLISH YOUR M.I.N.S. TODAY?   ☐ YES   ☐ NO

TODAY'S WINS

_____

_____

_____

TODAY I STRUGGLED WITH

_____

_____

_____

OPPORTUNITIES FOR IMPROVEMENT:
SCALE OF 1-10 HOW PRODUCTIVE WERE YOU TODAY?

PLANS FOR TOMORROW:

NOTES

DAILY PLAN

JAN FEB MAR APR MAY JUN JUL AUG SEP OCT NOV DEC
1 2 3 4 5 6 7 8 9 10 11 12 13 14 15 16 17 18 19 20 21 22 23 24 25 26 27 28 29 30 31

MORNING ROUTINE

THREE THINGS I AM GRATEFUL FOR:

_____

_____

_____

THREE THINGS I AM EXCITED FOR:

_____

_____

_____

WOKE UP: _____   HOURS SLEPT: _____   HIT SNOOZE? ▪Y ▪N

FOCUS	TODAY'S PT	REJUVENATE

GOAL #1
WEEKLY OBJECTIVE:
M.I.N.S.:

GOAL #2
WEEKLY OBJECTIVE:
M.I.N.S.:

GOAL #3
WEEKLY OBJECTIVE:
M.I.N.S.:

IF I DO THESE THREE THINGS TODAY I WILL WIN THE DAY!

1 _____

2 _____

3 _____

TIME BLOCKING

0400 _____	1000 _____	1600 _____
0430 _____	1030 _____	1630 _____
0500 _____	1100 _____	1700 _____
0530 _____	1130 _____	1730 _____
0600 _____	1200 _____	1800 _____
0630 _____	1230 _____	1830 _____
0700 _____	1300 _____	1900 _____
0730 _____	1330 _____	1930 _____
0800 _____	1400 _____	2000 _____
0830 _____	1430 _____	2030 _____
0900 _____	1500 _____	2100 _____
0930 _____	1530 _____	2130 _____

SCHEDULE ENOUGH BREAKS? ☐   SCHEDULED M.I.N.S ☐

EVENING REVIEW

DID YOU ACCOMPLISH YOUR M.I.N.S. TODAY?   ☐ YES   ☐ NO

TODAY'S WINS

_____

_____

_____

TODAY I STRUGGLED WITH

_____

_____

_____

OPPORTUNITIES FOR IMPROVEMENT:
SCALE OF 1-10 HOW PRODUCTIVE WERE YOU TODAY? _____

PLANS FOR TOMORROW:

NOTES

DAILY PLAN

JAN FEB MAR APR MAY JUN JUL AUG SEP OCT NOV DEC
1 2 3 4 5 6 7 8 9 10 11 12 13 14 15 16 17 18 19 20 21 22 23 24 25 26 27 28 29 30 31

MORNING ROUTINE

THREE THINGS I AM GRATEFUL FOR:

_____

_____

_____

THREE THINGS I AM EXCITED FOR:

_____

_____

_____

WOKE UP: _____   HOURS SLEPT: _____   HIT SNOOZE? ☐ Y ☐ N

FOCUS	TODAY'S PT	REJUVENATE

GOAL #1 _____
WEEKLY OBJECTIVE:
M.I.N.S.:

GOAL #2 _____
WEEKLY OBJECTIVE:
M.I.N.S.:

GOAL #3 _____
WEEKLY OBJECTIVE:
M.I.N.S.:

IF I DO THESE THREE THINGS TODAY I WILL WIN THE DAY!

1. _____
2. _____
3. _____

TIME BLOCKING

0400 _____	1000 _____	1600 _____
0430 _____	1030 _____	1630 _____
0500 _____	1100 _____	1700 _____
0530 _____	1130 _____	1730 _____
0600 _____	1200 _____	1800 _____
0630 _____	1230 _____	1830 _____
0700 _____	1300 _____	1900 _____
0730 _____	1330 _____	1930 _____
0800 _____	1400 _____	2000 _____
0830 _____	1430 _____	2030 _____
0900 _____	1500 _____	2100 _____
0930 _____	1530 _____	2130 _____

SCHEDULE ENOUGH BREAKS? ☐   SCHEDULED M.I.N.S ☐

EVENING REVIEW

DID YOU ACCOMPLISH YOUR M.I.N.S. TODAY?   ☐ YES   ☐ NO

TODAY'S WINS

_____
_____
_____

TODAY I STRUGGLED WITH

_____
_____
_____

OPPORTUNITIES FOR IMPROVEMENT:
SCALE OF 1-10 HOW PRODUCTIVE WERE YOU TODAY?

PLANS FOR TOMORROW:

NOTES

DAILY PLAN

JAN FEB MAR APR MAY JUN JUL AUG SEP OCT NOV DEC
1 2 3 4 5 6 7 8 9 10 11 12 13 14 15 16 17 18 19 20 21 22 23 24 25 26 27 28 29 30 31

MORNING ROUTINE

THREE THINGS I AM GRATEFUL FOR:

_____

_____

_____

THREE THINGS I AM EXCITED FOR:

_____

_____

_____

WOKE UP: _____   HOURS SLEPT: _____   HIT SNOOZE? ☐ Y ☐ N

FOCUS	TODAY'S PT	REJUVENATE

GOAL #1
WEEKLY OBJECTIVE:
M.I.N.S.:

GOAL #2
WEEKLY OBJECTIVE:
M.I.N.S.:

GOAL #3
WEEKLY OBJECTIVE:
M.I.N.S.:

IF I DO THESE THREE THINGS TODAY I WILL WIN THE DAY!

1 _____

2 _____

3 _____

TIME BLOCKING

0400 _____	1000 _____	1600 _____
0430 _____	1030 _____	1630 _____
0500 _____	1100 _____	1700 _____
0530 _____	1130 _____	1730 _____
0600 _____	1200 _____	1800 _____
0630 _____	1230 _____	1830 _____
0700 _____	1300 _____	1900 _____
0730 _____	1330 _____	1930 _____
0800 _____	1400 _____	2000 _____
0830 _____	1430 _____	2030 _____
0900 _____	1500 _____	2100 _____
0930 _____	1530 _____	2130 _____

SCHEDULE ENOUGH BREAKS? ☐   SCHEDULED M.I.N.S ☐

EVENING REVIEW

DID YOU ACCOMPLISH YOUR M.I.N.S. TODAY?   ☐ YES   ☐ NO

TODAY'S WINS

_____

_____

_____

TODAY I STRUGGLED WITH

_____

_____

_____

OPPORTUNITIES FOR IMPROVEMENT:
SCALE OF 1-10 HOW PRODUCTIVE WERE YOU TODAY?

PLANS FOR TOMORROW:

NOTES

DAILY PLAN

JAN FEB MAR APR MAY JUN JUL AUG SEP OCT NOV DEC
1 2 3 4 5 6 7 8 9 10 11 12 13 14 15 16 17 18 19 20 21 22 23 24 25 26 27 28 29 30 31

MORNING ROUTINE

THREE THINGS I AM GRATEFUL FOR:

_____

_____

_____

THREE THINGS I AM EXCITED FOR:

_____

_____

_____

WOKE UP: _____   HOURS SLEPT: _____   HIT SNOOZE? ■Y ■N

FOCUS	TODAY'S PT	REJUVENATE

GOAL #1
WEEKLY OBJECTIVE:
M.I.N.S.:

GOAL #2
WEEKLY OBJECTIVE:
M.I.N.S.:

GOAL #3
WEEKLY OBJECTIVE:
M.I.N.S.:

IF I DO THESE THREE THINGS TODAY I WILL WIN THE DAY!

1. _____
2. _____
3. _____

TIME BLOCKING

0400 _____	1000 _____	1600 _____
0430 _____	1030 _____	1630 _____
0500 _____	1100 _____	1700 _____
0530 _____	1130 _____	1730 _____
0600 _____	1200 _____	1800 _____
0630 _____	1230 _____	1830 _____
0700 _____	1300 _____	1900 _____
0730 _____	1330 _____	1930 _____
0800 _____	1400 _____	2000 _____
0830 _____	1430 _____	2030 _____
0900 _____	1500 _____	2100 _____
0930 _____	1530 _____	2130 _____

SCHEDULE ENOUGH BREAKS? ☐   SCHEDULED M.I.N.S ☐

EVENING REVIEW

DID YOU ACCOMPLISH YOUR M.I.N.S. TODAY?   ☐ YES   ☐ NO

TODAY'S WINS

_____

_____

_____

TODAY I STRUGGLED WITH

_____

_____

_____

OPPORTUNITIES FOR IMPROVEMENT:
SCALE OF 1-10 HOW PRODUCTIVE WERE YOU TODAY?

PLANS FOR TOMORROW:

NOTES

DAILY PLAN

JAN FEB MAR APR MAY JUN JUL AUG SEP OCT NOV DEC
1 2 3 4 5 6 7 8 9 10 11 12 13 14 15 16 17 18 19 20 21 22 23 24 25 26 27 28 29 30 31

MORNING ROUTINE

THREE THINGS I AM
GRATEFUL FOR:

_____

_____

_____

THREE THINGS I AM
EXCITED FOR:

_____

_____

_____

WOKE UP: _____   HOURS SLEPT: _____   HIT SNOOZE? ▪Y ▪N

FOCUS	TODAY'S PT	REJUVENATE

GOAL #1 _____
WEEKLY OBJECTIVE:
M.I.N.S.:

GOAL #2 _____
WEEKLY OBJECTIVE:
M.I.N.S.:

GOAL #3 _____
WEEKLY OBJECTIVE:
M.I.N.S.:

IF I DO THESE THREE THINGS TODAY I WILL WIN THE DAY!

1 _____

2 _____

3 _____

TIME BLOCKING

0400	1000	1600
0430	1030	1630
0500	1100	1700
0530	1130	1730
0600	1200	1800
0630	1230	1830
0700	1300	1900
0730	1330	1930
0800	1400	2000
0830	1430	2030
0900	1500	2100
0930	1530	2130

SCHEDULE ENOUGH BREAKS? ▢   SCHEDULED M.I.N.S ▢

EVENING REVIEW

DID YOU ACCOMPLISH YOUR M.I.N.S. TODAY?   ▢ YES   ▢ NO

TODAY'S WINS

_____

_____

_____

TODAY I STRUGGLED WITH

_____

_____

_____

OPPORTUNITIES FOR IMPROVEMENT:
SCALE OF 1-10 HOW PRODUCTIVE WERE YOU TODAY?

PLANS FOR TOMORROW:

NOTES

DAILY PLAN

JAN FEB MAR APR MAY JUN JUL AUG SEP OCT NOV DEC
1 2 3 4 5 6 7 8 9 10 11 12 13 14 15 16 17 18 19 20 21 22 23 24 25 26 27 28 29 30 31

MORNING ROUTINE

THREE THINGS I AM GRATEFUL FOR:

_____

_____

_____

THREE THINGS I AM EXCITED FOR:

_____

_____

_____

WOKE UP: _____   HOURS SLEPT: _____   HIT SNOOZE? ■ Y ■ N

FOCUS	TODAY'S PT	REJUVENATE

GOAL #1 _____
WEEKLY OBJECTIVE:
M.I.N.S.:

GOAL #2 _____
WEEKLY OBJECTIVE:
M.I.N.S.:

GOAL #3 _____
WEEKLY OBJECTIVE:
M.I.N.S.:

IF I DO THESE THREE THINGS TODAY I WILL WIN THE DAY!

1. _____
2. _____
3. _____

TIME BLOCKING

0400	1000	1600
0430	1030	1630
0500	1100	1700
0530	1130	1730
0600	1200	1800
0630	1230	1830
0700	1300	1900
0730	1330	1930
0800	1400	2000
0830	1430	2030
0900	1500	2100
0930	1530	2130

SCHEDULE ENOUGH BREAKS? ☐   SCHEDULED M.I.N.S ☐

EVENING REVIEW

DID YOU ACCOMPLISH YOUR M.I.N.S. TODAY?   ☐ YES   ☐ NO

TODAY'S WINS

_____

_____

_____

TODAY I STRUGGLED WITH

_____

_____

_____

OPPORTUNITIES FOR IMPROVEMENT:
SCALE OF 1-10 HOW PRODUCTIVE WERE YOU TODAY?

PLANS FOR TOMORROW:

NOTES

DAILY PLAN

JAN FEB MAR APR MAY JUN JUL AUG SEP OCT NOV DEC
1 2 3 4 5 6 7 8 9 10 11 12 13 14 15 16 17 18 19 20 21 22 23 24 25 26 27 28 29 30 31

MORNING ROUTINE

THREE THINGS I AM GRATEFUL FOR:

_____

_____

_____

THREE THINGS I AM EXCITED FOR:

_____

_____

_____

WOKE UP: _____   HOURS SLEPT: _____   HIT SNOOZE? ☐ Y ☐ N

FOCUS	TODAY'S PT	REJUVENATE

GOAL #1 _____
WEEKLY OBJECTIVE:
M.I.N.S.:

GOAL #2 _____
WEEKLY OBJECTIVE:
M.I.N.S.:

GOAL #3 _____
WEEKLY OBJECTIVE:
M.I.N.S.:

IF I DO THESE THREE THINGS TODAY I WILL WIN THE DAY!

1. _____

2. _____

3. _____

TIME BLOCKING

0400 _____	1000 _____	1600 _____
0430 _____	1030 _____	1630 _____
0500 _____	1100 _____	1700 _____
0530 _____	1130 _____	1730 _____
0600 _____	1200 _____	1800 _____
0630 _____	1230 _____	1830 _____
0700 _____	1300 _____	1900 _____
0730 _____	1330 _____	1930 _____
0800 _____	1400 _____	2000 _____
0830 _____	1430 _____	2030 _____
0900 _____	1500 _____	2100 _____
0930 _____	1530 _____	2130 _____

SCHEDULE ENOUGH BREAKS? ☐   SCHEDULED M.I.N.S ☐

EVENING REVIEW

DID YOU ACCOMPLISH YOUR M.I.N.S. TODAY?   ☐ YES   ☐ NO

TODAY'S WINS

_____

_____

_____

TODAY I STRUGGLED WITH

_____

_____

_____

OPPORTUNITIES FOR IMPROVEMENT:
SCALE OF 1-10 HOW PRODUCTIVE WERE YOU TODAY?

PLANS FOR TOMORROW:

NOTES

DAILY PLAN

JAN FEB MAR APR MAY JUN JUL AUG SEP OCT NOV DEC
1 2 3 4 5 6 7 8 9 10 11 12 13 14 15 16 17 18 19 20 21 22 23 24 25 26 27 28 29 30 31

MORNING ROUTINE

THREE THINGS I AM GRATEFUL FOR:

_____

_____

_____

THREE THINGS I AM EXCITED FOR:

_____

_____

_____

WOKE UP: _____ HOURS SLEPT: _____ HIT SNOOZE? ■Y ■N

FOCUS	TODAY'S PT	REJUVENATE

GOAL #1 _____
WEEKLY OBJECTIVE:
M.I.N.S.:

GOAL #2 _____
WEEKLY OBJECTIVE:
M.I.N.S.:

GOAL #3 _____
WEEKLY OBJECTIVE:
M.I.N.S.:

IF I DO THESE THREE THINGS TODAY I WILL WIN THE DAY!

1 _____

2 _____

3 _____

TIME BLOCKING

0400 _____	1000 _____	1600 _____
0430 _____	1030 _____	1630 _____
0500 _____	1100 _____	1700 _____
0530 _____	1130 _____	1730 _____
0600 _____	1200 _____	1800 _____
0630 _____	1230 _____	1830 _____
0700 _____	1300 _____	1900 _____
0730 _____	1330 _____	1930 _____
0800 _____	1400 _____	2000 _____
0830 _____	1430 _____	2030 _____
0900 _____	1500 _____	2100 _____
0930 _____	1530 _____	2130 _____

SCHEDULE ENOUGH BREAKS? ☐   SCHEDULED M.I.N.S ☐

EVENING REVIEW

DID YOU ACCOMPLISH YOUR M.I.N.S. TODAY?   ☐ YES   ☐ NO

TODAY'S WINS

_____

_____

_____

TODAY I STRUGGLED WITH

_____

_____

_____

OPPORTUNITIES FOR IMPROVEMENT:
SCALE OF 1-10 HOW PRODUCTIVE WERE YOU TODAY?

PLANS FOR TOMORROW:

NOTES

DAILY PLAN

JAN FEB MAR APR MAY JUN JUL AUG SEP OCT NOV DEC
1 2 3 4 5 6 7 8 9 10 11 12 13 14 15 16 17 18 19 20 21 22 23 24 25 26 27 28 29 30 31

MORNING ROUTINE

THREE THINGS I AM GRATEFUL FOR:

_____

_____

_____

THREE THINGS I AM EXCITED FOR:

_____

_____

_____

WOKE UP: _____   HOURS SLEPT: _____   HIT SNOOZE? ■Y ■N

FOCUS	TODAY'S PT	REJUVENATE

GOAL #1
WEEKLY OBJECTIVE:
M.I.N.S.:

GOAL #2
WEEKLY OBJECTIVE:
M.I.N.S.:

GOAL #3
WEEKLY OBJECTIVE:
M.I.N.S.:

IF I DO THESE THREE THINGS TODAY I WILL WIN THE DAY!

1 _____

2 _____

3 _____

TIME BLOCKING

0400 _____	1000 _____	1600 _____
0430 _____	1030 _____	1630 _____
0500 _____	1100 _____	1700 _____
0530 _____	1130 _____	1730 _____
0600 _____	1200 _____	1800 _____
0630 _____	1230 _____	1830 _____
0700 _____	1300 _____	1900 _____
0730 _____	1330 _____	1930 _____
0800 _____	1400 _____	2000 _____
0830 _____	1430 _____	2030 _____
0900 _____	1500 _____	2100 _____
0930 _____	1530 _____	2130 _____

SCHEDULE ENOUGH BREAKS? ▢   SCHEDULED M.I.N.S ▢

EVENING REVIEW

DID YOU ACCOMPLISH YOUR M.I.N.S. TODAY?   ▢ YES   ▢ NO

TODAY'S WINS

_____

_____

_____

TODAY I STRUGGLED WITH

_____

_____

_____

OPPORTUNITIES FOR IMPROVEMENT:
SCALE OF 1-10 HOW PRODUCTIVE WERE YOU TODAY?

PLANS FOR TOMORROW:

NOTES

DAILY PLAN

JAN   FEB   MAR   APR   MAY   JUN   JUL   AUG   SEP   OCT   NOV   DEC
1 2 3 4 5 6 7 8 9 10 11 12 13 14 15 16 17 18 19 20 21 22 23 24 25 26 27 28 29 30 31

MORNING ROUTINE

THREE THINGS I AM GRATEFUL FOR:

_____

_____

_____

THREE THINGS I AM EXCITED FOR:

_____

_____

_____

WOKE UP: _____   HOURS SLEPT: _____   HIT SNOOZE? ■ Y ■ N

FOCUS	TODAY'S PT	REJUVENATE

GOAL #1 _____
WEEKLY OBJECTIVE:
M.I.N.S.:

GOAL #2 _____
WEEKLY OBJECTIVE:
M.I.N.S.:

GOAL #3 _____
WEEKLY OBJECTIVE:
M.I.N.S.:

IF I DO THESE THREE THINGS TODAY I WILL WIN THE DAY!

1 _____

2 _____

3 _____

TIME BLOCKING

0400 _____	1000 _____	1600 _____
0430 _____	1030 _____	1630 _____
0500 _____	1100 _____	1700 _____
0530 _____	1130 _____	1730 _____
0600 _____	1200 _____	1800 _____
0630 _____	1230 _____	1830 _____
0700 _____	1300 _____	1900 _____
0730 _____	1330 _____	1930 _____
0800 _____	1400 _____	2000 _____
0830 _____	1430 _____	2030 _____
0900 _____	1500 _____	2100 _____
0930 _____	1530 _____	2130 _____

SCHEDULE ENOUGH BREAKS? ☐   SCHEDULED M.I.N.S ☐

EVENING REVIEW

DID YOU ACCOMPLISH YOUR M.I.N.S. TODAY?   ☐ YES   ☐ NO

TODAY'S WINS

_____
_____
_____

TODAY I STRUGGLED WITH

_____
_____
_____

OPPORTUNITIES FOR IMPROVEMENT:
SCALE OF 1-10 HOW PRODUCTIVE WERE YOU TODAY? _____

PLANS FOR TOMORROW:

NOTES

DAILY PLAN

JAN   FEB   MAR   APR   MAY   JUN   JUL   AUG   SEP   OCT   NOV   DEC
1 2 3 4 5 6 7 8 9 10 11 12 13 14 15 16 17 18 19 20 21 22 23 24 25 26 27 28 29 30 31

MORNING ROUTINE

THREE THINGS I AM GRATEFUL FOR:

_____

_____

_____

THREE THINGS I AM EXCITED FOR:

_____

_____

_____

WOKE UP: _____   HOURS SLEPT: _____   HIT SNOOZE? ▪Y ▪N

FOCUS	TODAY'S PT	REJUVENATE

GOAL #1
WEEKLY OBJECTIVE:
M.I.N.S.:

GOAL #2
WEEKLY OBJECTIVE:
M.I.N.S.:

GOAL #3
WEEKLY OBJECTIVE:
M.I.N.S.:

IF I DO THESE THREE THINGS TODAY I WILL WIN THE DAY!

1 _____

2 _____

3 _____

TIME BLOCKING

0400 _____	1000 _____	1600 _____
0430 _____	1030 _____	1630 _____
0500 _____	1100 _____	1700 _____
0530 _____	1130 _____	1730 _____
0600 _____	1200 _____	1800 _____
0630 _____	1230 _____	1830 _____
0700 _____	1300 _____	1900 _____
0730 _____	1330 _____	1930 _____
0800 _____	1400 _____	2000 _____
0830 _____	1430 _____	2030 _____
0900 _____	1500 _____	2100 _____
0930 _____	1530 _____	2130 _____

SCHEDULE ENOUGH BREAKS? ▢   SCHEDULED M.I.N.S ▢

EVENING REVIEW

DID YOU ACCOMPLISH YOUR M.I.N.S. TODAY?   ▢ YES   ▢ NO

TODAY'S WINS   **TODAY I STRUGGLED WITH**

_____   _____

_____   _____

_____   _____

OPPORTUNITIES FOR IMPROVEMENT:
SCALE OF 1-10 HOW PRODUCTIVE WERE YOU TODAY?

PLANS FOR TOMORROW: **NOTES**

DAILY PLAN

JAN FEB MAR APR MAY JUN JUL AUG SEP OCT NOV DEC
1 2 3 4 5 6 7 8 9 10 11 12 13 14 15 16 17 18 19 20 21 22 23 24 25 26 27 28 29 30 31

MORNING ROUTINE

THREE THINGS I AM GRATEFUL FOR:

_____

_____

_____

THREE THINGS I AM EXCITED FOR:

_____

_____

_____

WOKE UP: _____   HOURS SLEPT: _____   HIT SNOOZE? ■ Y ■ N

FOCUS	TODAY'S PT	REJUVENATE

GOAL #1 _____
WEEKLY OBJECTIVE:
M.I.N.S.:

GOAL #2 _____
WEEKLY OBJECTIVE:
M.I.N.S.:

GOAL #3 _____
WEEKLY OBJECTIVE:
M.I.N.S.:

IF I DO THESE THREE THINGS TODAY I WILL WIN THE DAY!

1 _____

2 _____

3 _____

TIME BLOCKING

0400	1000	1600
0430	1030	1630
0500	1100	1700
0530	1130	1730
0600	1200	1800
0630	1230	1830
0700	1300	1900
0730	1330	1930
0800	1400	2000
0830	1430	2030
0900	1500	2100
0930	1530	2130

SCHEDULE ENOUGH BREAKS? ☐   SCHEDULED M.I.N.S ☐

EVENING REVIEW

DID YOU ACCOMPLISH YOUR M.I.N.S. TODAY?   ☐ YES   ☐ NO

TODAY'S WINS

_____

_____

_____

TODAY I STRUGGLED WITH

_____

_____

_____

OPPORTUNITIES FOR IMPROVEMENT:
SCALE OF 1-10 HOW PRODUCTIVE WERE YOU TODAY?

PLANS FOR TOMORROW:

NOTES

DAILY PLAN

JAN   FEB   MAR   APR   MAY   JUN   JUL   AUG   SEP   OCT   NOV   DEC
1 2 3 4 5 6 7 8 9 10 11 12 13 14 15 16 17 18 19 20 21 22 23 24 25 26 27 28 29 30 31

MORNING ROUTINE

THREE THINGS I AM GRATEFUL FOR:

_____

_____

_____

THREE THINGS I AM EXCITED FOR:

_____

_____

_____

WOKE UP: _____   HOURS SLEPT: _____   HIT SNOOZE? ■Y ■N

FOCUS	TODAY'S PT	REJUVENATE

GOAL #1
WEEKLY OBJECTIVE:
M.I.N.S.:

GOAL #2
WEEKLY OBJECTIVE:
M.I.N.S.:

GOAL #3
WEEKLY OBJECTIVE:
M.I.N.S.:

IF I DO THESE THREE THINGS TODAY I WILL WIN THE DAY!

1. _____
2. _____
3. _____

TIME BLOCKING

0400	1000	1600
0430	1030	1630
0500	1100	1700
0530	1130	1730
0600	1200	1800
0630	1230	1830
0700	1300	1900
0730	1330	1930
0800	1400	2000
0830	1430	2030
0900	1500	2100
0930	1530	2130

SCHEDULE ENOUGH BREAKS? ☐   SCHEDULED M.I.N.S ☐

EVENING REVIEW

DID YOU ACCOMPLISH YOUR M.I.N.S. TODAY?   ☐ YES   ☐ NO

TODAY'S WINS

_____

_____

_____

TODAY I STRUGGLED WITH

_____

_____

_____

OPPORTUNITIES FOR IMPROVEMENT:
SCALE OF 1-10 HOW PRODUCTIVE WERE YOU TODAY?

PLANS FOR TOMORROW:

NOTES

DAILY PLAN

JAN FEB MAR APR MAY JUN JUL AUG SEP OCT NOV DEC
1 2 3 4 5 6 7 8 9 10 11 12 13 14 15 16 17 18 19 20 21 22 23 24 25 26 27 28 29 30 31

MORNING ROUTINE

THREE THINGS I AM GRATEFUL FOR:

_____

_____

_____

THREE THINGS I AM EXCITED FOR:

_____

_____

_____

WOKE UP: _____   HOURS SLEPT: _____   HIT SNOOZE? ▪Y ▪N

FOCUS	TODAY'S PT	REJUVENATE

GOAL #1 _____
WEEKLY OBJECTIVE:
M.I.N.S.:

GOAL #2 _____
WEEKLY OBJECTIVE:
M.I.N.S.:

GOAL #3 _____
WEEKLY OBJECTIVE:
M.I.N.S.:

IF I DO THESE THREE THINGS TODAY I WILL WIN THE DAY!

1 _____

2 _____

3 _____

TIME BLOCKING

0400 _____	1000 _____	1600 _____
0430 _____	1030 _____	1630 _____
0500 _____	1100 _____	1700 _____
0530 _____	1130 _____	1730 _____
0600 _____	1200 _____	1800 _____
0630 _____	1230 _____	1830 _____
0700 _____	1300 _____	1900 _____
0730 _____	1330 _____	1930 _____
0800 _____	1400 _____	2000 _____
0830 _____	1430 _____	2030 _____
0900 _____	1500 _____	2100 _____
0930 _____	1530 _____	2130 _____

SCHEDULE ENOUGH BREAKS? ☐   SCHEDULED M.I.N.S ☐

EVENING REVIEW

DID YOU ACCOMPLISH YOUR M.I.N.S. TODAY?   ☐ YES   ☐ NO

TODAY'S WINS

_____

_____

_____

TODAY I STRUGGLED WITH

_____

_____

_____

OPPORTUNITIES FOR IMPROVEMENT:
SCALE OF 1-10 HOW PRODUCTIVE WERE YOU TODAY? _____

PLANS FOR TOMORROW:

NOTES

DAILY PLAN

JAN FEB MAR APR MAY JUN JUL AUG SEP OCT NOV DEC
1 2 3 4 5 6 7 8 9 10 11 12 13 14 15 16 17 18 19 20 21 22 23 24 25 26 27 28 29 30 31

MORNING ROUTINE

THREE THINGS I AM GRATEFUL FOR:

_____

_____

_____

THREE THINGS I AM EXCITED FOR:

_____

_____

_____

WOKE UP: _____   HOURS SLEPT: _____   HIT SNOOZE? ▪Y ▪N

FOCUS	TODAY'S PT	REJUVENATE

GOAL #1
WEEKLY OBJECTIVE:
M.I.N.S.:

GOAL #2
WEEKLY OBJECTIVE:
M.I.N.S.:

GOAL #3
WEEKLY OBJECTIVE:
M.I.N.S.:

IF I DO THESE THREE THINGS TODAY I WILL WIN THE DAY!

1 _____

2 _____

3 _____

TIME BLOCKING

0400	1000	1600
0430	1030	1630
0500	1100	1700
0530	1130	1730
0600	1200	1800
0630	1230	1830
0700	1300	1900
0730	1330	1930
0800	1400	2000
0830	1430	2030
0900	1500	2100
0930	1530	2130

SCHEDULE ENOUGH BREAKS? ☐ SCHEDULED M.I.N.S ☐

EVENING REVIEW

DID YOU ACCOMPLISH YOUR M.I.N.S. TODAY?   ☐ YES   ☐ NO

TODAY'S WINS

_____

_____

_____

TODAY I STRUGGLED WITH

_____

_____

_____

OPPORTUNITIES FOR IMPROVEMENT:
SCALE OF 1-10 HOW PRODUCTIVE WERE YOU TODAY?

PLANS FOR TOMORROW:

NOTES

DAILY PLAN

JAN FEB MAR APR MAY JUN JUL AUG SEP OCT NOV DEC
1 2 3 4 5 6 7 8 9 10 11 12 13 14 15 16 17 18 19 20 21 22 23 24 25 26 27 28 29 30 31

MORNING ROUTINE

THREE THINGS I AM GRATEFUL FOR:

_____

_____

_____

THREE THINGS I AM EXCITED FOR:

_____

_____

_____

WOKE UP: _____   HOURS SLEPT: _____   HIT SNOOZE? ■Y ■N

FOCUS	TODAY'S PT	REJUVENATE

GOAL #1 _____
WEEKLY OBJECTIVE:
M.I.N.S.:

GOAL #2 _____
WEEKLY OBJECTIVE:
M.I.N.S.:

GOAL #3 _____
WEEKLY OBJECTIVE:
M.I.N.S.:

IF I DO THESE THREE THINGS TODAY I WILL WIN THE DAY!

1 _____

2 _____

3 _____

TIME BLOCKING

0400 _____	1000 _____	1600 _____
0430 _____	1030 _____	1630 _____
0500 _____	1100 _____	1700 _____
0530 _____	1130 _____	1730 _____
0600 _____	1200 _____	1800 _____
0630 _____	1230 _____	1830 _____
0700 _____	1300 _____	1900 _____
0730 _____	1330 _____	1930 _____
0800 _____	1400 _____	2000 _____
0830 _____	1430 _____	2030 _____
0900 _____	1500 _____	2100 _____
0930 _____	1530 _____	2130 _____

SCHEDULE ENOUGH BREAKS? ▢   SCHEDULED M.I.N.S ▢

EVENING REVIEW

DID YOU ACCOMPLISH YOUR M.I.N.S. TODAY?   ▢ YES   ▢ NO

TODAY'S WINS

_____
_____
_____

TODAY I STRUGGLED WITH

_____
_____
_____

OPPORTUNITIES FOR IMPROVEMENT:
SCALE OF 1-10 HOW PRODUCTIVE WERE YOU TODAY? _____

PLANS FOR TOMORROW:

NOTES

DAILY PLAN

JAN FEB MAR APR MAY JUN JUL AUG SEP OCT NOV DEC
1 2 3 4 5 6 7 8 9 10 11 12 13 14 15 16 17 18 19 20 21 22 23 24 25 26 27 28 29 30 31

MORNING ROUTINE

THREE THINGS I AM GRATEFUL FOR:

_____

_____

_____

THREE THINGS I AM EXCITED FOR:

_____

_____

_____

WOKE UP: _____   HOURS SLEPT: _____   HIT SNOOZE? ▪Y ▪N

FOCUS	TODAY'S PT	REJUVENATE

GOAL #1 _____
WEEKLY OBJECTIVE:
M.I.N.S.:

GOAL #2 _____
WEEKLY OBJECTIVE:
M.I.N.S.:

GOAL #3 _____
WEEKLY OBJECTIVE:
M.I.N.S.:

IF I DO THESE THREE THINGS TODAY I WILL WIN THE DAY!

1. _____
2. _____
3. _____

TIME BLOCKING

0400 _____	1000 _____	1600 _____
0430 _____	1030 _____	1630 _____
0500 _____	1100 _____	1700 _____
0530 _____	1130 _____	1730 _____
0600 _____	1200 _____	1800 _____
0630 _____	1230 _____	1830 _____
0700 _____	1300 _____	1900 _____
0730 _____	1330 _____	1930 _____
0800 _____	1400 _____	2000 _____
0830 _____	1430 _____	2030 _____
0900 _____	1500 _____	2100 _____
0930 _____	1530 _____	2130 _____

SCHEDULE ENOUGH BREAKS? ☐   SCHEDULED M.I.N.S ☐

EVENING REVIEW

DID YOU ACCOMPLISH YOUR M.I.N.S. TODAY?   ☐ YES   ☐ NO

TODAY'S WINS

_____

_____

_____

TODAY I STRUGGLED WITH

_____

_____

_____

OPPORTUNITIES FOR IMPROVEMENT: _____

SCALE OF 1-10 HOW PRODUCTIVE WERE YOU TODAY? _____

PLANS FOR TOMORROW:

NOTES

DAILY PLAN

JAN FEB MAR APR MAY JUN JUL AUG SEP OCT NOV DEC
1 2 3 4 5 6 7 8 9 10 11 12 13 14 15 16 17 18 19 20 21 22 23 24 25 26 27 28 29 30 31

MORNING ROUTINE

THREE THINGS I AM GRATEFUL FOR:

_____

_____

_____

THREE THINGS I AM EXCITED FOR:

_____

_____

_____

WOKE UP: _____   HOURS SLEPT: _____   HIT SNOOZE? ■Y ■N

FOCUS	TODAY'S PT	REJUVENATE

GOAL #1 _____
WEEKLY OBJECTIVE:
M.I.N.S.:

GOAL #2 _____
WEEKLY OBJECTIVE:
M.I.N.S.:

GOAL #3 _____
WEEKLY OBJECTIVE:
M.I.N.S.:

IF I DO THESE THREE THINGS TODAY I WILL WIN THE DAY!

1 _____

2 _____

3 _____

TIME BLOCKING

0400	1000	1600
0430	1030	1630
0500	1100	1700
0530	1130	1730
0600	1200	1800
0630	1230	1830
0700	1300	1900
0730	1330	1930
0800	1400	2000
0830	1430	2030
0900	1500	2100
0930	1530	2130

SCHEDULE ENOUGH BREAKS? ☐   SCHEDULED M.I.N.S ☐

EVENING REVIEW

DID YOU ACCOMPLISH YOUR M.I.N.S. TODAY?   ☐ YES   ☐ NO

TODAY'S WINS

_____

_____

_____

TODAY I STRUGGLED WITH

_____

_____

_____

OPPORTUNITIES FOR IMPROVEMENT:
SCALE OF 1-10 HOW PRODUCTIVE WERE YOU TODAY?

PLANS FOR TOMORROW:

NOTES

DAILY PLAN

JAN FEB MAR APR MAY JUN JUL AUG SEP OCT NOV DEC
1 2 3 4 5 6 7 8 9 10 11 12 13 14 15 16 17 18 19 20 21 22 23 24 25 26 27 28 29 30 31

MORNING ROUTINE

THREE THINGS I AM GRATEFUL FOR:

_____

_____

_____

THREE THINGS I AM EXCITED FOR:

_____

_____

_____

WOKE UP: _____   HOURS SLEPT: _____   HIT SNOOZE? ■ Y ■ N

FOCUS	TODAY'S PT	REJUVENATE

GOAL #1
WEEKLY OBJECTIVE:
M.I.N.S.:

GOAL #2
WEEKLY OBJECTIVE:
M.I.N.S.:

GOAL #3
WEEKLY OBJECTIVE:
M.I.N.S.:

IF I DO THESE THREE THINGS TODAY I WILL WIN THE DAY!

1. _____
2. _____
3. _____

TIME BLOCKING

0400 _____	1000 _____	1600 _____
0430 _____	1030 _____	1630 _____
0500 _____	1100 _____	1700 _____
0530 _____	1130 _____	1730 _____
0600 _____	1200 _____	1800 _____
0630 _____	1230 _____	1830 _____
0700 _____	1300 _____	1900 _____
0730 _____	1330 _____	1930 _____
0800 _____	1400 _____	2000 _____
0830 _____	1430 _____	2030 _____
0900 _____	1500 _____	2100 _____
0930 _____	1530 _____	2130 _____

SCHEDULE ENOUGH BREAKS? ☐   SCHEDULED M.I.N.S ☐

EVENING REVIEW

DID YOU ACCOMPLISH YOUR M.I.N.S. TODAY?   ☐ YES   ☐ NO

TODAY'S WINS

_____
_____
_____

TODAY I STRUGGLED WITH

_____
_____
_____

OPPORTUNITIES FOR IMPROVEMENT:
SCALE OF 1-10 HOW PRODUCTIVE WERE YOU TODAY?

PLANS FOR TOMORROW:

NOTES

DAILY PLAN

JAN FEB MAR APR MAY JUN JUL AUG SEP OCT NOV DEC
1 2 3 4 5 6 7 8 9 10 11 12 13 14 15 16 17 18 19 20 21 22 23 24 25 26 27 28 29 30 31

MORNING ROUTINE

THREE THINGS I AM GRATEFUL FOR:

_____

_____

_____

THREE THINGS I AM EXCITED FOR:

_____

_____

_____

WOKE UP: _____   HOURS SLEPT: _____   HIT SNOOZE? ■Y ■N

FOCUS	TODAY'S PT	REJUVENATE

GOAL #1
WEEKLY OBJECTIVE:
M.I.N.S.:

GOAL #2
WEEKLY OBJECTIVE:
M.I.N.S.:

GOAL #3
WEEKLY OBJECTIVE:
M.I.N.S.:

IF I DO THESE THREE THINGS TODAY I WILL WIN THE DAY!

1 _____

2 _____

3 _____

TIME BLOCKING

0400	1000	1600
0430	1030	1630
0500	1100	1700
0530	1130	1730
0600	1200	1800
0630	1230	1830
0700	1300	1900
0730	1330	1930
0800	1400	2000
0830	1430	2030
0900	1500	2100
0930	1530	2130

SCHEDULE ENOUGH BREAKS? ☐   SCHEDULED M.I.N.S ☐

EVENING REVIEW

DID YOU ACCOMPLISH YOUR M.I.N.S. TODAY?   ☐ YES   ☐ NO

TODAY'S WINS

_____

_____

_____

TODAY I STRUGGLED WITH

_____

_____

_____

OPPORTUNITIES FOR IMPROVEMENT:
SCALE OF 1-10 HOW PRODUCTIVE WERE YOU TODAY?

PLANS FOR TOMORROW:

NOTES

DAILY PLAN

JAN FEB MAR APR MAY JUN JUL AUG SEP OCT NOV DEC
1 2 3 4 5 6 7 8 9 10 11 12 13 14 15 16 17 18 19 20 21 22 23 24 25 26 27 28 29 30 31

MORNING ROUTINE

THREE THINGS I AM GRATEFUL FOR:

_____

_____

_____

THREE THINGS I AM EXCITED FOR:

_____

_____

_____

WOKE UP: _____   HOURS SLEPT: _____   HIT SNOOZE? ▪Y ▪N

FOCUS	TODAY'S PT	REJUVENATE

GOAL #1 _____
WEEKLY OBJECTIVE:
M.I.N.S.:

GOAL #2 _____
WEEKLY OBJECTIVE:
M.I.N.S.:

GOAL #3 _____
WEEKLY OBJECTIVE:
M.I.N.S.:

IF I DO THESE THREE THINGS TODAY I WILL WIN THE DAY!

1. _____
2. _____
3. _____

TIME BLOCKING

0400 _____	1000 _____	1600 _____
0430 _____	1030 _____	1630 _____
0500 _____	1100 _____	1700 _____
0530 _____	1130 _____	1730 _____
0600 _____	1200 _____	1800 _____
0630 _____	1230 _____	1830 _____
0700 _____	1300 _____	1900 _____
0730 _____	1330 _____	1930 _____
0800 _____	1400 _____	2000 _____
0830 _____	1430 _____	2030 _____
0900 _____	1500 _____	2100 _____
0930 _____	1530 _____	2130 _____

SCHEDULE ENOUGH BREAKS? ☐   SCHEDULED M.I.N.S ☐

EVENING REVIEW

DID YOU ACCOMPLISH YOUR M.I.N.S. TODAY?   ☐ YES   ☐ NO

TODAY'S WINS

_____

_____

_____

TODAY I STRUGGLED WITH

_____

_____

_____

OPPORTUNITIES FOR IMPROVEMENT:
SCALE OF 1-10 HOW PRODUCTIVE WERE YOU TODAY?

PLANS FOR TOMORROW:

NOTES

DAILY PLAN

JAN FEB MAR APR MAY JUN JUL AUG SEP OCT NOV DEC
1 2 3 4 5 6 7 8 9 10 11 12 13 14 15 16 17 18 19 20 21 22 23 24 25 26 27 28 29 30 31

MORNING ROUTINE

THREE THINGS I AM GRATEFUL FOR:

_____

_____

_____

THREE THINGS I AM EXCITED FOR:

_____

_____

_____

WOKE UP: _____   HOURS SLEPT: _____   HIT SNOOZE? ▪Y ▪N

FOCUS	TODAY'S PT	REJUVENATE

GOAL #1 _____
WEEKLY OBJECTIVE:
M.I.N.S.:

GOAL #2 _____
WEEKLY OBJECTIVE:
M.I.N.S.:

GOAL #3 _____
WEEKLY OBJECTIVE:
M.I.N.S.:

IF I DO THESE THREE THINGS TODAY I WILL WIN THE DAY!

1. _____
2. _____
3. _____

TIME BLOCKING

0400	1000	1600
0430	1030	1630
0500	1100	1700
0530	1130	1730
0600	1200	1800
0630	1230	1830
0700	1300	1900
0730	1330	1930
0800	1400	2000
0830	1430	2030
0900	1500	2100
0930	1530	2130

SCHEDULE ENOUGH BREAKS? ☐   SCHEDULED M.I.N.S ☐

EVENING REVIEW

DID YOU ACCOMPLISH YOUR M.I.N.S. TODAY?   ☐ YES   ☐ NO

TODAY'S WINS

_____

_____

_____

TODAY I STRUGGLED WITH

_____

_____

_____

OPPORTUNITIES FOR IMPROVEMENT:
SCALE OF 1-10 HOW PRODUCTIVE WERE YOU TODAY?

PLANS FOR TOMORROW:

NOTES

DAILY PLAN

JAN FEB MAR APR MAY JUN JUL AUG SEP OCT NOV DEC
1 2 3 4 5 6 7 8 9 10 11 12 13 14 15 16 17 18 19 20 21 22 23 24 25 26 27 28 29 30 31

MORNING ROUTINE

THREE THINGS I AM GRATEFUL FOR:

_____

_____

_____

THREE THINGS I AM EXCITED FOR:

_____

_____

_____

WOKE UP: _____ HOURS SLEPT: _____ HIT SNOOZE? ☐ Y ☐ N

FOCUS	TODAY'S PT	REJUVENATE

GOAL #1
WEEKLY OBJECTIVE:
M.I.N.S.:

GOAL #2
WEEKLY OBJECTIVE:
M.I.N.S.:

GOAL #3
WEEKLY OBJECTIVE:
M.I.N.S.:

IF I DO THESE THREE THINGS TODAY I WILL WIN THE DAY!

1 _____

2 _____

3 _____

TIME BLOCKING

0400	1000	1600
0430	1030	1630
0500	1100	1700
0530	1130	1730
0600	1200	1800
0630	1230	1830
0700	1300	1900
0730	1330	1930
0800	1400	2000
0830	1430	2030
0900	1500	2100
0930	1530	2130

SCHEDULE ENOUGH BREAKS? ☐   SCHEDULED M.I.N.S ☐

EVENING REVIEW

DID YOU ACCOMPLISH YOUR M.I.N.S. TODAY?   ☐ YES   ☐ NO

TODAY'S WINS

_____

_____

_____

TODAY I STRUGGLED WITH

_____

_____

_____

OPPORTUNITIES FOR IMPROVEMENT:
SCALE OF 1-10 HOW PRODUCTIVE WERE YOU TODAY?

PLANS FOR TOMORROW:

NOTES

DAILY PLAN

JAN FEB MAR APR MAY JUN JUL AUG SEP OCT NOV DEC
1 2 3 4 5 6 7 8 9 10 11 12 13 14 15 16 17 18 19 20 21 22 23 24 25 26 27 28 29 30 31

MORNING ROUTINE

THREE THINGS I AM GRATEFUL FOR:

_____

_____

_____

THREE THINGS I AM EXCITED FOR:

_____

_____

_____

WOKE UP: _____ HOURS SLEPT: _____ HIT SNOOZE? ■ Y ■ N

FOCUS	TODAY'S PT	REJUVENATE

GOAL #1
WEEKLY OBJECTIVE:
M.I.N.S.:

GOAL #2
WEEKLY OBJECTIVE:
M.I.N.S.:

GOAL #3
WEEKLY OBJECTIVE:
M.I.N.S.:

IF I DO THESE THREE THINGS TODAY I WILL WIN THE DAY!

1. _____

2. _____

3. _____

TIME BLOCKING

0400	1000	1600
0430	1030	1630
0500	1100	1700
0530	1130	1730
0600	1200	1800
0630	1230	1830
0700	1300	1900
0730	1330	1930
0800	1400	2000
0830	1430	2030
0900	1500	2100
0930	1530	2130

SCHEDULE ENOUGH BREAKS? ☐   SCHEDULED M.I.N.S ☐

EVENING REVIEW

DID YOU ACCOMPLISH YOUR M.I.N.S. TODAY?   ☐ YES   ☐ NO

TODAY'S WINS

_____

_____

_____

TODAY I STRUGGLED WITH

_____

_____

_____

OPPORTUNITIES FOR IMPROVEMENT:
SCALE OF 1-10 HOW PRODUCTIVE WERE YOU TODAY?

PLANS FOR TOMORROW:

NOTES

HABIT TRACKER

HABITS   1   2   3   4   5   6   7   8   9   10   11

_____

_____

_____

_____

_____

_____

_____

_____

_____

_____

WEEKLY HABITS

HABITS	W1	W2	W3	W4	W5

MONTH _____

12 13 14 15 16 17 18 19 20 21 22 23 24 25 26 27 28 29 30 31

MONTHLY HABITS

NOTES

HABIT TRACKER

HABITS   1 2 3 4 5 6 7 8 9 10 11

_____

_____

_____

_____

_____

_____

_____

_____

_____

_____

WEEKLY HABITS

HABITS	W1	W2	W3	W4	W5

MONTH _____

12 13 14 15 16 17 18 19 20 21 22 23 24 25 26 27 28 29 30 31

MONTHLY HABITS

NOTES

HABIT TRACKER

HABITS 1 2 3 4 5 6 7 8 9 10 11

_____

_____

_____

_____

_____

_____

_____

_____

_____

_____

WEEKLY HABITS

HABITS	W1	W2	W3	W4	W5

MONTH _____

12 13 14 15 16 17 18 19 20 21 22 23 24 25 26 27 28 29 30 31

MONTHLY HABITS

- _____
- _____
- _____
- _____
- _____
- _____
- _____
- _____
- _____
- _____

NOTES

THE THREE P'S

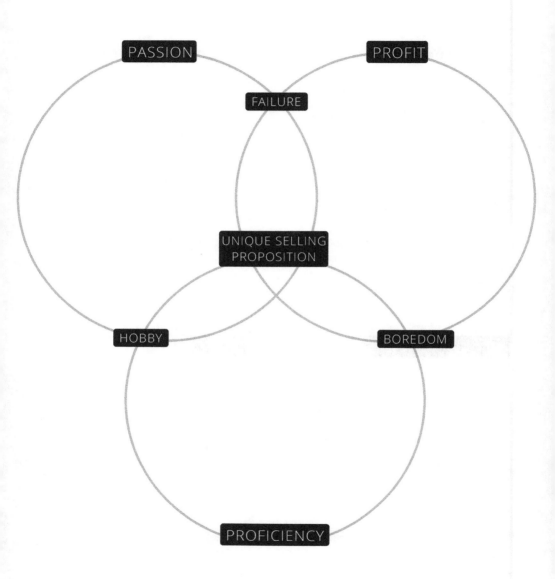

CONNECT WITH THE
MILITARY MILLIONAIRE COMMUNITY

AND ACHIEVE THE FINANCIAL FREEDOM YOU DESERVE!

 @frommilitarytomillionaire   /david-pere

 /groups/militarymillionaire   @militarymillionaire

P.S. If you enjoyed this book, it would mean a lot to me if you would leave an honest review on Amazon.

Scan here to leave a review!

www.frommilitarytomillionaire.com

FREE RESOURCES

Would you like help finding a realtor for your area? Let me and my team help connect you with a vetted, talented real estate agent: **https://www.frommilitarytomillionaire.com/va-realtor/** (Using the same link, we can also refer you to a recommended VA lender for your area if you would like!)

For a list of books I recommend, check out my constantly updated reading list: **https://www.frommilitarytomillionaire.com/kit**

The Military Millionaire Podcast:
https://www.frommilitarytomillionaire.com/podcast/

Join the Facebook Group:
https://www.facebook.com/groups/militarymillionaire/

Instagram:
https://www.instagram.com/frommilitarytomillionaire/

YouTube Channel:
https://www.frommilitarytomillionaire.com/youtube

VA loan video playlist:
https://www.frommilitarytomillionaire.com/va-loan-videos

Want to get on the email list that is dedicated specifically to investment opportunities? Fill out this short form at our investment portal: **https://www.frommilitarytomillionaire.com/investors/**

PREMIUM RESOURCES

From Zero to One: Real Estate Investing for Beginners (course):
https://www.frommilitarytomillionaire.com/teachable-rei

Finding Off-Market Real Estate Deals (course):
https://www.frommilitarytomillionaire.com/teachable-off-market

Apply for the War Room Real Estate Mastermind:
https://www.frommilitarytomillionaire.com/mastermind-application/

For a complete list of resources:
https://www.frommilitarytomillionaire.com/resources/